SAVE PERFECTION FOR

Heaven

Stevie,
Rejoice
in the design.

JANA CONRAD
Phil 1:30,31

SAVE PERFECTION FOR

Heaven

down to earth interior design

JANA CONRAD

A Division of WINEPRESS PUBLISHING

ISBN 1-4141-0334-4
Library of Congress Catalog Card Number: 2004099622

Acknowledgements

Julie Crum – Mom, you taught me about God every day of my life and told me I could do whatever God wanted me to do.

James Conrad – you have been unselfish in letting me work on this book while you helped with the house and the kids. Most husbands would not be so flexible – it is the best gift you have ever given me.

Kenley, Marina, and Cooper – you helped me find the time to get it done - the very best kids in the whole world!

Steven Crum – as my little brother, you were my first answer to prayer. As an adult, you are one of the kindest men I know.

Nell Conrad – you reared a son who is a wonderful husband and father.

Kelly Wishart – for your never-ending challenge to keep on top of what I am doing and for your friendship I am thankful.

Tim and Deb Abramowitz – your immediate friendship and the desire to follow God's principles in your lives makes me appreciate you every day.

Tim and Devona Tarbell – your friendship and guidance through the years are priceless.

Dawna Underwood – your skill helped shape this book into what it should be grammatically and practically.

Monya Mollohan – you did a beautiful job of capturing my style in the book cover.

Vicki Hubbard – you challenged me from the day I met you to reach higher than I thought I could.

Don and Sue Wilson – your mentoring and your leadership of our church have always been a motivation to me. You challenge me to have a spirit of excellence and determination to tell people about what God has done in my life.

Jack Cavanaugh – your input was invaluable and your encouragement kept me going.

Deborah Edwards – God has given you a talent for capturing His creation on film. You have a true passion for your gift– thanks for sharing your photography with this ministry.

Harold Crum – Dad, you pointed me in the direction of my Heavenly Father – best thing that ever happened in my life.

Northwest Christian School Cheerleaders – thanks for keeping me young!

God – the Ultimate Designer – this book is dedicated to His glory.

*A special thanks to Dr. Brian Easley and Dr. Bradley Storks for your professional input on how God created our bodies to respond to His design.

*Photography provided by Deborah Edwards ilvphotos@cox.net

*Scripture is NIV and KJV

Introduction

The room is warm and alive with color and texture. Thought provoking details are scattered throughout, enticing one to openly examine every corner. Stacks of books arranged to look as though they are actually useful line the coffee table where a vase of fresh flowers takes center stage. Light gracefully filters through the high arched windows making a lovely silhouette of the curved banister in the foyer. Only marble and granite cover the floors and countertops and the imported fabrics are most likely from France. Two women speak in soft tones enjoying each other's company over a cup of coffee.

"My, what a wonderful place," one sighs.

"It is enjoyable," the second one confesses. "I can't stay for long. I have to go pick up the kids from school."

"Me too, I almost forgot. It's easy to get caught up in the moment!"

Both women venture around the dwelling a few more moments and then leave the model home to go back to ten-year-old couches, walls that have never thought about being painted, bookshelves crammed with everything under the sun – a glaring difference to the perfectly decorated, never lived-in look of the model home.

It is amusing to go into the kids' room in a model home. They have two stuffed animals sitting politely on the bed and the latest fabrics in the cutest kid prints – no expense has been spared. There are no fingerprints on the light switches and the dresser tops are clear except for the three knick-knacks the decorator picked out to go on top of the dresser. There are no socks or underwear lying behind the bathroom door. Need I say more?

This may be the world we would like to live in, but it is a far cry from the reality that belongs to those of us who answer to "Honey" or "Mom." So what is decorating to us who find ourselves in the category of "attached" to other human beings?

"...And before the throne there was ...a sea of glass like crystal." (Rev. 4:6a)

Now that's perfection! But it should be – it's heaven. With the God-given desire to make pretty homes, some of us need to be encouraged that we do not need to be an expert to accomplish the task. This side of heaven, decorating is not about perfection. (Did I hear a sigh of relief?) Decorating is also not about buying expensive things for your home or getting rid of everything you possess and starting over. It is not about competing with your neighbor or your best friend and most importantly it is **not** hard to do!

It is about the five senses with which God equipped us. It is about pleasing our eyes, ears, nose, mouth and hands. It is about enjoying life to the fullest. For this reason, none of our homes look exactly alike, and because it is about how we as individuals enjoy life, EVERYONE can decorate. How can I say that everyone can decorate and be sure I am right? Because of what it says in Genesis 1:27, "So God created man in his own image." Since you were created in the image of God and He is the author of design – then you absolutely have some level of design ability – don't take my word for it – take His. Enjoy, be creative, and remember – **Save Perfection for Heaven!**

TABLE OF CONTENTS

Part Two
The Creatures of Design (Creation day 6)

Part Three
The Creator of Design

Chapter 1

A New Beginning

The lady of the house opens the door and smiles. The interior designer she hired is here – the savior of the undecorated. She has waited anxiously for this day - after years of living with unpainted, unpapered, and unaccessorized rooms! The designer swoops in with her color wheel and fabric swatches and looks distastefully at the furniture.

"This will all have to go!" she screeches. "My painter will be here tomorrow at 8:00 a.m. sharp, and I will have the most elaborate new design for your room, unlike any you have ever seen. The fabrics are imported, the paint is Ralph Lauren; the furniture is the most expensive money can buy. You can rest assured you will have the most decorated, the most glamorously beautiful room ever created. Crowds will come from miles around just to get a glance at your room. *People* magazine will want an interview, and the *Lifestyles of the Rich and Famous* photographer will be here to immortalize it on film."

She finishes her speech and is gone. The lady of the house is almost too excited for words. She calls all her friends to tell them about the design project. "Come to my house next week for brunch and you can view my new room. Only those with exquisite taste will truly understand how wonderful it will be."

The day is finally here. She has a room like no other. It is perfectly decorated with the most exquisite fabrics and furniture. It is a place to entertain even the most prestigious person. Movie stars may even call her to find out where she bought her sofa. She stands outside the door with a number of family members and friends. They chat excitedly until the designer pulls into the driveway and trots up the steps. Everyone becomes respectfully silent. The moment has arrived.

The designer welcomes everyone saying, "I assume that everyone here will be able to appreciate this level of design. Not everyone can, you know. Some are too simple to understand true design. I hope no one here will be left out of the enjoyment because of their own lack of good taste." The designer finishes her speech and then opens the door.

The lady of the house enters her new room followed by the mob in her front yard. She "oohs" and "aahs" over the colors and the furniture. "It's exquisite," she says to her husband. "The finest of fabrics, so I'm told."

The decorator explains all of the most important pieces while everyone exclaims over the room.

"She is one of the most respected decorators around," one person comments reassuring everyone that they also know and understand good taste. Secretly she is unconvinced that the room looks good, but everyone else seems to think the room is wonderful.

All of the adults continue to compliment the design, embarrassed by their own apparent lack of taste, for they find the room rather distasteful. Just then the owner's son returns from school. The seven-year-old stands in the doorway of the living room. His eyebrows knit and his nose wrinkles.

"This looks awful," he says to no one in particular. "That couch looks like it came out of Grandma's closet. You hate the way Grandma dresses. They painted the room gold. You hate the color gold." Looking into his mother's crimson face he says, "Take my advice, Mom; next time maybe you should consult me before you change the room. I can remind you of what you really like so you don't make this mistake again."

Designer's Workshop:

The television decorating show host exuberantly says, "You can do it!" and another smiles and declares her ideas are "A good thing." But how can we be sure they're right? After all, they don't know how badly we can mess things up! They have had years to perfect the trade of interior design and we have had only moments spliced together between the rigors of real life. And who do we side with? One has an idea and someone else another. Who is right? What if we make a mistake! What if we make a horrible blunder of decorating and break one of those decorating rules that only interior design people can tell you but everyone else can see?

Let's talk about model homes for a moment. Aren't they beautiful? How would you like to learn how to make your home look just like one of those homes? Let me ask you another question, who lives in those model homes? Who picks up the dirty underwear behind the door? Who are these people who have only three things in their pantry, no clothes in their closets and no junk mail on their counters? How about those children who are content to play with only three toys and leave their little knick-knacks on the dresser alone? Sure, their table is always set, but nobody ever enjoys sitting down to eat in that dining room. Let's take a closer look at life for a moment.

As we walk through life what keeps our tongues from saying: your tag is sticking up, your slip is showing, your deodorant stopped working, and you have lipstick on your teeth? We are so good at noticing the details. Why do we hesitate when it comes to telling a person something that will help them? I'll tell you why. We want to pretend we live in a perfect world.

As women we know what we want and more importantly, we know what we don't want. We want to be liked, but more importantly we don't want to be disliked. We want to be heard and understood, but we don't want to be talked about behind our backs. We don't want to have a physical flaw, but if we do we want to be thought of as beautiful by someone. We want to be thought of as kind, but we don't want to always be kind. We want to have friends but we don't want to have to always be friendly. We want to be married, but more importantly we do not want to be alone. We want to always be right, but more importantly we want to never be wrong. If I could sum up in one word what women want it is – *perfection.*

Girls are excellent mimics. We want our homes to look like the picture in the magazine and stay that way all day long even though we have three kids, a dog and a husband. I would like to clean the kitchen and then never cook again so that it will always look new. We bring home the new table to use and then spend all our time making it look like it was never used at all. We want everything to stay looking new. It is a human trait, a very old human trait. Adam and Eve had to leave the Garden of Eden, but they did not forget what it was like to live in Eden. Things had changed, but I imagine they tried to make it feel like what they had thought of as "home."

I can hear Eve saying to Adam, "Get that weed out of the front yard, it came back! I'll have no weeds in this yard, do you hear me! We didn't have to live with them before, and I'm certainly not going to put up with them now. And one more thing, that tree looks lopsided – fix it. If there is one thing I know, it's how a tree is supposed to look and there is something wrong with that one."

We want things done perfectly, but a lot of us women are not "do-it-yourself" people. So we have to hire another perfectionist to do the actual work. We want a perfect house, perfect kids, and perfect pets. Some of us can't handle pets in the house because in order for a pet to be in the house it has to smell perfectly, play perfectly, and "potty" perfectly, and if it can't – out it goes. At times we barely tolerate our kids making mistakes - who needs to put up with an animal?

To step out and tell a person something she needs to hear makes her uncomfortable, but more than that, it shatters our image of a pretty world. We like our pretense. We settle nicely into our shallow, unimportant conversation and enjoy the fantasy played out from every picture of adulthood we have ever entertained. We like "dress up" and tea parties. We romanticize the bygone days of ladies with parasols and gloved hands – days filled with women sitting in the parlor having quiet conversations. While doing needlepoint, they wait for their suitor to come calling, hoping he will carry them across the threshold of his southern mansion. In reality, we know those days were filled with hard chores for most, but the instinct is still there – to sit quietly by with a polite smile and a partially sincere, "How do you do?" Whether we lack the strength to be a true friend, or the guts to decorate and have someone criticize it, both ruin our endeavor to pretend life is perfect. It's easier to leave it alone than to change it and risk ridicule.

Let's look at the "rules" of interior design. Whose rules will determine the direction to go? I found a "rule" a while ago that has served me very nicely when it comes to interior design, so let's start with that rule. Here it is - Stop following all the rules! Design is supposed to be creative and different. Our society seems to be chasing after a few people's ideas of what looks good. How can something be different if everything is the same? Decorating is not about being normal. Many people want to decorate so they can move from plain and ordinary to status quo. Those who really want to make a statement want to make it perfectly, so they never even start.

What I really want you to do is to think like a designer. If you understand the reasoning behind the "rules" you never have to follow the rules again. Some of you are totally uninhibited in the decorating of your homes – good for you. Keep at it,

> Designer thinking: It doesn't matter how you play the game. It is whether you win or lose that counts.

and maybe apply some of that same creative thinking to other areas of your lives.

Designer thinking says: *It doesn't matter how you play the game, it's whether you win or lose that counts!* Designer thinking may not be true in everyday life, but in the design world it is most definitely true. It does not matter how you accomplish the look of your room, it only matters that it turns out to be a winner. I want to clarify that last part – it only matters that it turns out a winner – to you! If the president of the association of interior designers herself comes into your room and says it doesn't work – but you like it – then it works! I know someone out there is saying, "Well, I haven't decorated and that works for me." This brings up a few good questions:

- What is decorating and why do we do it?
- Who are the people who usually decorate?
- What if I am not like them? Can I still learn to decorate?

WHY DO WE DECORATE?

Decorating has always been symbolic. From the ancient Egyptian pyramids to the White House as it is today, decorating exhibits:

- What we believe
- What motivates us
- What and who we honor
- Where we have been
- What we have discovered
- Who has influenced us

The White House, which was first occupied in 1800, is a good example of the symbolism that is a part of decorating. In 1962 Mrs. Kennedy chose a green fabric that was set aside until they used it for the 1971 makeover of the room that is appropriately called the "Green Room." They found a de-

> Ceramic bowls of the landing on the moon were made to commemorate July 20, 1969. People proudly put them in their homes.

sign for the window treatments in an early 1900's magazine and used a fabric of beige, green, and coral striped satin. They placed golden American eagles with wings outstretched over the top of each window. A key word for what goes into a decorating project is – sentiment! Merriam-Webster defines sentiment as "An idea colored by emotion."[1] This brings us to our next question.

WHAT IS DECORATING?

Not only is decorating **symbolic,** it also encompasses our **entire human experience.** It is:

- Social
- Emotional
- External and internal
- Physical
- Mental
- Spiritual

We decorate to accommodate our own level of social activity. If you entertain people in your home, you plan for their needs. Seating, extra glassware, and stocked available bathrooms are good examples of how someone who takes a social approach to decorating considers her decorating project.

Someone who takes a physical approach to decorating will have available the things someone might need! Here are some things they might have available: extra pillows, blankets, wash cloths, towels, nightlights, cots, extra brushes, food, and of course, conversation.

Throughout the book we will discover how these six areas: physical, mental, spiritual, internal/external, emotional, and so-cial, directly affect our own outlook on decorating and coincide with our five senses. My desire is to encourage and motivate you to decorate the way that is best suited to your own personality, abilities, and needs.

Who is generally thought of as a decorator?

The most common belief is that the types of people who decorate are:

- Creative
- Driven
- Confident
- Talented
- Educated

So what happens to those of us who feel:

- Uneducated
- Stupid
- Reluctant

- Unimaginative
- Unmotivated

We will learn how everyone can decorate, and answer one more question – What should be our main motive in decorating? We will also take a closer look at you, by asking you two questions in this book:

1. What kind of woman are you?
2. What do you want?

Knowing the answer to these questions will lead you to a better understanding of how to accomplish the task of decorating your home with your personality. And remember: EVERYONE can decorate! How can I say that everyone can decorate and be sure I am right? Because of what it says in Genesis 1:27, "So God created man in his own image." Since you were created in the image of God and He is the author of design – then you absolutely have some level of design ability. Don't take my word for it – take His.

Jana's Decorating Personality Test

Choose the box that best describes you. Choose only one box per line. Remember that this is only an estimate of your stylistic tendencies. Although you should complete this test now, Chapter 3 will help you decipher it.

	Family One: Blue/grey	Family Two: Red/orange	Family Three: Black/neutrals
What is your favorite color family?	Family One: Blue/grey	Family Two: Red/orange	Family Three: Black/neutrals
What is your favorite shape?	Oval	Triangle	Square
What is your least favorite color?	Orange	Mauve	Yellow
What is the prominent color in your closet?	Blue or pink	Green or red	Black or tan
How many pairs of black shoes do you own?	1–3	0–10	7–10
Do you own a pair of red shoes?	Yes, but I don't wear them.	Yes!	No!
Do you tend to be:	Sensitive	Friendly	Determined
What are the colors of your everyday dishes?	Blue, cream or pink	Multicolored	Black, white or beige
How many extra pillows do you have on your couch?	5–10	3–4	0–2
When choosing a picture which of these are you most inclined to choose?	Landscapes/History	Animals/People	Abstract shapes
When choosing between old things or brand new you:	Love old things	Love old and new	Love new Hate old
You tend to be:	Faithful	Outgoing	Practical
In fabrics you tend to choose:	Florals/Solids/plaids	Solids/Geometrics	Stripes/Solids
Do you like to dress up and go out?	Yes	Yes and no	Go out—yes Dress up—no
Is your kitchen table	Oval	Square	Rectangle

A New Beginning

What color is your car?	Blue	Red	Black
How long ago did you replace your towels?	5 years or more	3–5 years	0–2 years
You tend to be:	Reflective	Talkative	Decisive
How many pieces of furniture are in your living room?	5–12	7–14	2–5
Have you ever picked up something someone else threw away?	Yes	Yes!	No!
Do you shop at secondhand stores?	Yes!	Sure, why not?	No!
Do you buy the top of the line?	No!	I don't know	Yes
Do you like the color yellow?	No	Sure	Is that a color?
You tend to be:	Feeling deeply	Impractical	Strong willed

PART ONE

The Creation of Design

Psalm 77:14 says, "You are the God who performs miracles; you display your power among the people."

Seeing is Believing

(Creation Day One)

I tend to enjoy looking for broken things when I go shopping, because I like to fix them. My mother does not enjoy the prospect of having to fix something in order for it to be useable. She only shops for things that are ready to go. You have your own particular likes and dislikes that will make your room distinctive. You will be looking at your own preferences in a new way while we go through the steps of design as laid out in the Bible. One of the questions many people ask me is, "What style am I?" I hate to put people in a box based on what someone else has named a "style." For the most part I don't believe anyone to be just one "style," but we seem to need a place to start, so here is my gauge for what "style" you might be.

Designer's Workshop:

> If you like pretty things, you're Victorian.
> If you like cute things, you're Country.

If you like ugly things, you're Gothic.
If you like things that clash, you're Country French.
If you like gaudy things, you're Rococo.
If you like things to be symmetrical, you're Traditional.
If you like things that are tropical and tranquil, you're Mediterranean.
If you like things smooth and fluid, you're Metropolitan.
If you like oriental things, you're Oriental.
If you like all of them, you're Eclectic.

Our quest to better understand decorating and how it relates to us and our five senses begins with our eyes. Sight is usually the first sense that detects the atmosphere in a room. Color, of course, is one of the main components for someone redecorating their room. However, it is only one of the elements of design, and we will be talking about color in depth at a later time.

I do have just one thing to say about color at this time: Many people drive themselves crazy trying to match colors exactly, or worry about putting colors together that "don't go." I doubt you get worked up and frustrated every morning when you choose your attire for the day - so don't worry about color in decorating either.

As I stated earlier, color is only one element of design that catches our eye. We are also drawn to different textures and shapes. Some people like things that are round or floral, while others like things that are geometric like squares and triangles. Aren't you glad God not only made the different shapes, but He made someone to like each of them? Think about the different shapes that appeal to you so that you can apply **Designer Thinking:** *"Beauty is in the eye of the beholder"* – as the saying goes. For the purpose of this book, we are going to apply it to our design projects. When you look

Designer Thinking: Beauty is in the eye of the beholder.

at a room, look for the elements you enjoy. You may be tempted to throw everything out and start over, but if you look carefully at each item you will find some things that are still beautiful to you, even if you have had them for twenty years. You may even find you are attracted to something you thought of as ugly – but you can picture it painted or recovered in some way and you are ready to transform it. The item has the same shape, but you have decided to change the look of the item to meet the new design needs. The shape is what attracted you – keep this in mind when you go shopping, especially if going to an antique store or second hand shop. It is easy to get bogged down when looking at so many things at a time, but when you are concentrating on shapes you enjoy, it becomes easier.

Keep in mind what you like and the general idea of what decorating is, and let's move forward to the bare essentials.

LET THERE BE LIGHT!

One of the bare essentials to decorating is light. Since there are no colors without light, and no textures unless you can make the distinction between surfaces, it makes sense that light is one of the main essentials in decorating. You will notice that light is the first thing God created in the decorating of the world. "And God said, 'Let there be light,' and there was light. God saw that the light was good, and he separated the light from the darkness" (Gen. 1:3-4).

As you view your room, decide how the room will be used and what kind of lighting you will need for the different spaces. Lighting can easily be broken down into three basic sections: overhead lighting, floor or accent lighting, and task lighting. Let's look at these three types of lighting.

Regarding **overhead lighting** - you usually just use what you have. It isn't very decorative, it's just functional - you walk into a room and turn on the light. Make sure the bulbs you use are the correct wattage. I use bulbs with the highest wattage recommended because I am looking for function. Dimming switches can be installed in places like family and living rooms, but are particularly effective in the dining room. This adds versatility to the atmosphere you desire to create. Some of the smaller spaces like bathrooms and hallways have lights that can be changed completely in order to update the space. This can make a big difference in the style of your room.

Floor and accent lighting is where you get to really have fun with atmosphere. These consist mostly of floor lamps, table lamps, and up lights. In most family and living rooms one floor lamp is plenty. Add one table lamp to these same rooms and this is where most people conclude their lighting mission. If you want to take lighting to the next level, try adding a few "up lights." These lights sit on the floor and shoot up behind a plant or couch. You can find them at Home Depot reasonably priced. When you apply this type of accent lighting you capture the ambiance that is present in the model homes you admire.

Task lighting is just as it sounds. If you have a desk, you need a desk light. If you have a sewing room you need extra light. Corners in the kitchen sometimes put your back to the main light. As a result, your shadow gives you a very dark working space. Lights under the cabinets solve this problem. Before you begin decorating, decide how you will use the room and what kind of lights you will need. Visit a lighting store and ask questions. The more questions you ask the more likely you are to save money and achieve the desired result.

We have started our decorating venture with actual light. There is another kind of light we need to address. We will define it as "clarity." In order to clarify what direction you want your space to go, you must start with what you have.

Work with what you have

Start with bare walls if you can. Take everything out of the room except the main pieces of furniture. For example, in the living room leave the couch and entertainment center. In the bedroom leave the bed and dresser. In the dining room leave the table. If you must, leave the curio cabinet or buffet table. In the bathroom, leave the commode and sink. Take out all the pictures, small end tables, coffee table, lamps, family photos, pillows, and Aunt Ida's Christmas gift from twenty-five years ago that never did match anything. Don't panic, I'll tell you what you can do with these items later. Take everything into a room where you can organize them and view them easily. Organize them into these three groups:

1. **Garage sale** – If you don't love it, get rid of it. Be honest with yourself about your possessions. Ask yourself when you last used or enjoyed the item. Here is a tip for what to do about Aunt Ida's Christmas gift of twenty-five years. If she notices it's gone say, "Aunt Ida, God wanted someone else to be blessed with it for the next twenty-five years." If you still feel the need to de-clutter but don't want to get rid of items for good, start a collection for your child by putting extra items into a Rubbermaid container with the child's name clearly marked. Then you can tell Aunt Ida you have put that item in a safe place to be passed down to little Sarah.

2. **Useable items** – these are the practical things you can't live without, like end tables and coffee makers. Now you will clearly be able to see the items that will definitely be returning to the room you are redecorating.

3. **Items with potential** – now is the time for you to use your "beauty is in the eye of the beholder" method. You may have looked at your possessions in a certain way for so long that it is hard to reinterpret them. Pretend you are at a garage sale looking at someone else's things. Think of new ways to use your items and voilà! you don't have to do so much shopping! Here are some questions to ask when looking at such items:

- Can I paint it?
- Can I cover it?
- Can I use it in a unique way?
- Can I change it somehow to get a different item altogether?
- Can I use it in another area of the house?

Get a friend who has the same ambition of redecorating and see if there are some things you can swap. Now it's getting fun!

After going through the multitude of items you've removed from the room you are redoing, return to the room that is going to be redecorated and get ready for the next phase of the process. (For those of you who are newly married or are not of the "packrat" persuasion, you may skip these last few steps and move along to the next.)

FABRIC AND LIGHT - WINDOWS

There are three reasons to use blinds.

1. Privacy
2. Light control
3. Beauty

Here are a few examples of blinds:

Wood blinds

Mini blinds

Plantation shutters

Vertical blinds

Cellular shades

> How to Measure for Blinds: Measure the inside window opening horizontally in three places: top, middle, and bottom. Measure the inside window opening vertically in two places: left and right.

There are no wrong decisions with blinds – so pick what you like. One of the most popular choices today is wood blinds, but in time that will change. As always, the key to decorating is keeping your eye open for changing times. Not that you have to jump up and transform things in your home every time styles change, but if you are in the process of renovating anyway, you may as well chose something up-to-date that will last for the next several years. Blinds can be an expensive investment so consider the cost. Get several estimates before purchasing and don't forget to ask the dealer if they are running a special. If they are not running a special, ask them if they will run one for you. Yes, you can do that—more often than people know! Tell them that if you are happy with their product and their customer service, you would be happy to pass out their business cards to your friends.

Fabrics

Fabric for windows is almost always used for beauty. However, it can be used for privacy and light control when the fabric is lined. It is cost effective to use a fabric panel that is pulled across the window at night for privacy and then pulled back from the window during the day to light the room. Your fabric is then serving two purposes, negating the use of blinds. This will bring down the price you pay for window coverings.

Choosing fabrics and patterns for your room is a crucial step in creating the look you desire. Don't forget, it is supposed to be fun, but sometimes it can be a chore. Here to help you is **Designer Thinking:** *make rash decisions.* How many times are you going to be told to make rash decisions?

> Designer Thinking: Make rash decisions - the first choice is usually the best choice.

Quite often the fabric the customer points out first is the one they end up choosing. At the fabric store view the fabrics from a distance. Take a closer look at the fabrics that catch your eye. You do not need to pick six or even four different fabrics. One printed fabric and one or two coordinating fabrics will be plenty for most rooms! One main fabric will decorate an entire room. If your couch is a patterned fabric instead of a solid, then your choice is already made for you (unless you choose to slipcover or replace the couch altogether). If you do plan to replace upholstered furniture, replace it before you do anything else. Usually only the main pieces will dictate the color scheme in a room – the couch, loveseat, bedspreads, etc.

Before you go to the fabric store decide what items will be staying the same and keep their patterns and colors in mind as you choose other fabrics to use in the room. I even cut off a very small piece of fabric from furniture from a discreet place to take with me to color match. This works very well, especially if you do not have an arm cover or loose pillow to take with you to represent the piece of furniture you are working around.

Patterns

How 'bout them patterns! If designers had a football team this is the one they would be rooting for - go Patterns go! The pattern you choose will begin the process of determining your style for that room. Most styles, however, can be "bent" several ways causing a room to be casual, semi-formal or formal. Don't worry about the choice of pattern. The style of the room will not be decided based on pattern alone. The components that complete style in a room are paint color and accessories.

The very first Designer chose fabric that was blue, scarlet, and purple when designing His Tabernacle. He had the patterns of cherubim woven into the fabric using gold thread. The fabric panels were 10 feet wide and hung on poles. Each fabric panel had fifty loops made out of blue linen. These loops were held together with gold clasps making the curtain continuous. The direction for this design was given to Moses by God two years after the Israelites' Exodus from Egypt somewhere around B.C. 1439. It is interesting that approximately 3500 years later people still think that purple, blue and red are great colors to decorate with, and some of our favorite accessories are angels.

Design Homework:

Review: Evaluate the lighting in the room you are decorating. How will you be using this area? What activities will be taking place in this space?

Remove: Take everything out of the room except the main pieces of furniture.

Regenerate: Find a place to display the removed items and set them up like a garage sale for yourself.

Refine: Go shopping at your own garage sale. Keep things that appeal to you just as they are. Make another pile of things that could be painted or renovated in some way. Make a last pile of what should go to the Salvation Army.

Realize: Go to a fabric store and view the fabrics from a distance – don't look too hard or long. Take a closer look in the section that first catches your eye. Back up and try again looking for another section that catches your eye – take a closer look. Collect swatches from three different sections that appeal to you – this will give you different options as you design. Take three samples from each section. Bring them home with you and put them in a journal or notebook that you can refer to as you work on your project.

Spiritual Workshop:

Let's look at another area not usually associated with design – your spiritual walk. Jesus said that out of the abundance of what is in our hearts, our mouths will speak (Matt. 12:34). What is true in our spiritual lives will be reflected in the decorating of our homes. If you have peace – your attitude will reflect peace in your home. If you have joy, it will be obvious in your home. And if you are lacking these, it will be equally noticeable to those who visit your home.

The goal in decorating is to create a space that reflects the attitudes, feelings, and comfort *you* desire. The rooms in your house are where you will be sharing time with your husband, reading to your children, and having quiet times with God.

When you are decorating the rooms in your home, you are imitating the Creator of the world. He gives you free reign to do this. There are no absolutes in His book for how you are to decorate your home – He wants the pleasure of seeing your creativity in action.

Can you imagine your six-year-old coming home from school and handing you a paper that another little boy made? You ask him with much interest why he brought home little Johnny's paper, and he answers, "Well, Mommy, I wanted you to have a really good paper, so I had Johnny make it for me to give you because he can draw better." What would you say to him? You would say, "But I want to see what YOU made! We cannot wait to see what our children create of their own making, and I imagine that our Heavenly Father feels very much the same about seeing us imitate His creativity in our homes. If we are going to use this God-given creativity in our homes, we will want to enter into it with the right spiritual perspective. How can we be spiritually ready to decorate? Let's look at a few ideas. These ideas will use the same principles as the decorating steps in this chapter. We will begin by using the principle:

"Work With What You Have" (spiritually)

In the spiritual world we must always begin right where we are. It makes no sense for a person to get well before going to the doctor, nor does it make sense to try and be "right" spiritually before we ask God to help us be right spiritually. Here are some steps for us to follow for our spiritual application:

Spiritual Homework:

1. **Review** how far you have come. Remember past victories and be encouraged to move further.

   Why do girls like to scream? I have two girls and both of them scream. They scream when they are happy, they scream when they are mad, they scream when they are excited. But then, life would be pretty boring if they just sat there. One day my younger daughter, who was three at the time, was running in a circle with the stance of a marathon runner searching for the finish line. I stood there as she passed me – she went on for several laps, so I asked her "Why are you running?" Without breaking her stride or even looking up she said, "I need to." I wish she would do that now instead of scream!

Why do people like to swing? You go back and forth on the seat and end up - nowhere. What is the fun in that? But it is fun, isn't it? Even as an adult I like to swing, and slide, and go on rides. We go for walks that lead us in a big circle back to our starting point with nothing gained but the walk itself – why?

Why do we find these sensations fun? Because we like to feel alive! We mark in our baby's book each new milestone and note the accomplishments in his life. Things like holding up his head, looking at his feet, and the arrival of his first tooth are all mile markers for proud parents. Smiling we say "You're getting to be such a big boy!" We find the enjoyment in living in the small things. They are the things that say "You're alive – enjoy!" The first day of kindergarten, your first love, and even your first break-up all weave together into the pattern of life. They make us who we are. So many variations make us unique. There are many different people in the world, each with their own set of milestones. What does God think about marking special times in our lives?

In the book of Joshua we find the account of God leading the Israelites across the Jordan River.

When the whole nation had finished crossing the Jordan, the Lord said to Joshua, "Choose twelve men from among the people, one from each tribe, and tell them to take up twelve stones from the middle of the Jordan from right where the priests stood and to carry them over with you and put them down at the place where you stay tonight."

So Joshua called together the twelve men he had ap-
pointed from the Israelites, one from each tribe, and said
to them, "Go over before the ark of the Lord your God
into the middle of the Jordan. Each of you is to take up
a stone on his shoulder, according to the number of the
tribes of the Israelites, to serve as a sign among you. In
the future, when your children ask you, "What do these
stones mean?" tell them that the flow of the Jordan was
cut off before the ark of the covenant of the Lord. When
it crossed the Jordan, the waters of the Jordan were cut
off. These stones are to be a memorial to the people of
Israel forever" (Joshua 4:1-7).

So it was God's idea for us to mark our milestones! (Do
I hear three cheers from the scrapbooking section?)

2. **Remove** unwanted items. Just as you clean out a room,
you can clean out the garbage of your spiritual life. You
might say, "How am I supposed to do that?" Start with
a spiritual inventory. If you find grumbling, ask God
to replace it with a thankful heart. "Rejoice in the Lord
always. I will say it again: Rejoice!" (Philippians 4:4).

If you find deceitfulness, ask God to replace it with
His truth, "All Scripture is God-breathed and is useful
for teaching, rebuking, correcting and training in righteousness, so that the man of God may be thoroughly
equipped for every good work" (2 Timothy 3:16, 17).

If you find a gossip's tongue, ask God to replace it with
words that lift up and encourage, "A word aptly spoken
is like apples of gold in settings of silver" (Proverbs
25:11).

Take this time to ask God if there is something in your life you need to remove in order to be used by Him.

3. **Regenerate** your enthusiasm. How? The Word of God. Psalm 119:105 says that God's Word is "A lamp to our feet and a light for our path." We have been talking about light in this chapter. Without light there are no colors. Without light we cannot see where we are heading. We need the light of God's Word to give us back our motivation to follow after God. The more we read and memorize God's Word the greater chance we will retain our enthusiasm for our relationship with God.

4. **Refine** your spiritual gifts. I Corinthians 12 tells us that God made us with different unique gifts to use for His glory.

5. **Realize** whether you have the "Light" in you. John said of Jesus, "Through him all things were made; without him nothing was made that has been made. In him was life, and that life was the light of men" (John 1:3, 4).

It is important for us to take this time to make sure we acknowledge that Jesus is the one and only way to get to heaven. We cannot perfect ourselves. This is another reason the title of this book is "Save Perfection for Heaven." We cannot get to heaven by ourselves any more than we have the ability to do anything perfectly on earth. We can try all we want - people have accomplished a lot of really grand things - but none of them are perfect. We will always be able to find a flaw. If you want things in line spiritually in your life, and you can't figure out what is missing, I encourage you to make sure you know Jesus as your Savior. It is His right to claim because He is the One who died on the cross for you, "But God demonstrates his own love for us in this: While we were still sinners, Christ died for us" (Romans 5:8). God promises, "That if you confess with your mouth, 'Jesus is Lord,' and believe in your heart that God raised him from the dead, you will be saved" (Romans 10:9).

Let's close by having you answer these two questions.

1. What does my home say about me?

2. What does my life say about me?

CHAPTER TWO RECIPE: HOW TO HAVE A "SAVE PERFECTION FOR HEAVEN" GARAGE SALE

One of the things that keep people from having garage sales is all the work it takes. Although we can't take all the work out of a sale, we can make it easier. Here are a few of my personal tips.

1. Don't mark the price on every item. Make a standard price for like items and make a sign with those prices listed. – (example: all kids' books .50 each)

2. With the rise of discount department stores, people are less inclined to pay the prices for garage sale clothing they were once willing to spend. Sell all clothing at your garage sale for .50 each. You will get rid of most of the clothing you don't need and your customers will have a great time. If you have any clothing that you feel should produce higher prices, try taking that group of clothing to a consignment shop.

3. Try to sell almost everything in your sale for no more than 10.00 each. If you have items that will bring a better price than 10.00—try selling them in the newspaper or on eBay.

4. Remember that the main reason for having a garage sale is to get rid of a lot of items. It is not to turn a profit—it is to try to regain some of the money you spent on these same items. Some people do make money having garage sales, but they do this as a business. If you try to make too much money, you will lose out on making the money you could have and you will be left still owning the items you were trying to be free from.

5. One way to save money is by not wasting money on advertising the sale in the paper. These ads cut into your

profit when it does not need to cost to help people know about your sale. Instead, make signs—don't put your address or advertise what you are selling on your signs. Just have your signs say "Sale" and include an arrow helping them to get to your house. The more signs you have, the more successful your sale will be. But the signs should be put within a three mile radius of your house. Don't bother putting them too far away.

6. Another way to make the sale fun and successful is to greet each person as they come and let them know this is their sale. Tell them that if they see anything they want—name their price, because you are trying to get rid of your stuff. Remember that your main desire is to get rid of your stuff. And the more fun you make the sale, the more people will buy from you.

7. Always offer to let them try electrical appliances to see if they work. Make sure to lower the price if they do not perform the way they should.

8. A successful sale to me, is when I get rid of 90% of my unwanted stuff and make between $200-400.

9. I usually have my sales on Saturday from 7am - 12. Believe it or not, that is all the time you need when you mark your things low. This also cuts down on the work usually required to have a sale.

10. The last hour of the sale I offer people a "bag" sale. Everything they can put in a bag for 3.00. And if I am really desperate to get rid of stuff I offer it for 1.00 a bag. If someone seems really interested in several of your books or a whole set of your baby clothes, offer them the whole box for $5-10. I have cleared off entire tables to one person using this technique. Good for them and good for you.

Psalm 71:19 says, "Your righteousness reaches to the skies, O God, you who have done great things."

THE SKY'S THE LIMIT

(Creation Day Two)

What's the worst that could happen? I ask myself as I stand atop a 24 foot extension ladder painting a client's house.

I could get off balance and fall spilling dark blue paint over their light colored carpet. I say back to myself!

That's right, and can you live with that? I ask myself.

Definitely not! I answer, and begin to waver in my desire to design or paint! I stand imagining the paint on the floor and the customer's less than happy demeanor when another thought surfaces.

Well, it's not like it's brain surgery – now if a surgeon makes a mistake – that's a mistake! But they keep on making important life decisions for other people everyday and this is just paint!

What a relief to hear you say that! I say to myself and resume painting. *Even if you were to completely mess up and spill the whole can of paint – the carpet can be replaced, the walls can be fixed – it isn't life-threatening! So the worst that can happen is that I may have to replace some carpet – can you live with that?* I ask myself.

Well, yes I can!

And so can I.

Designer's Workshop:

There is no limit to what you can do – unless you let fear get in your way. If you're an admirer of an imaginative person's decorating, you know she has put fear on the shelf while she decorates the rest of the room. Fear makes a lousy assistant.

> Designer Thinking: Fear makes a lousy assistant

Fear paralyzes and makes me focus on myself. Thoughts occur like, *Am I going to be embarrassed by this outcome?*

Someone once said, "The biggest mistake is the fear that you will make one." The greatest element in the things that embarrass us is fear. Fear is the undoing element - fear of what others will think of us.

As women, we have many fears, but the biggest one of all is – Shame! How will I look if I spill this entire can of paint? I will look foolish and incapable. What will they think of me if I say the wrong thing? They will think of me as uneducated.

One of the bad feelings Eve felt after eating the fruit in the Garden of Eden was shame. "Then the eyes of them both were opened, and they realized they were naked; so they sewed fig leaves together and made coverings for themselves" (Genesis 3:7). They made clothes because they felt ashamed.

Shame is a curse. Pain in childbearing is a curse also, but we overcome it with painkillers and epidurals. Weeds in our gardens are part of the curse, but they don't embarrass us – we just pull them. Tears are part of the fall of mankind from paradise but most women share them freely. So why are we afraid of shame?

Good questions! We will address this question in more detail a little later.

In this chapter we are going for the gold – unlimited creativity. If you are following the homework at the end of every chapter, you will have taken everything out of the room you are decorating and will be focusing on the specific use of that space in your home. It is time to reach for the stars. Think big – you may need to scale back later, but the bigger you allow yourself to dream, the more creative you will be with your design.

Ceiling and Walls

Here we stand looking at your ceiling and your walls – a blank slate. Some may be intimidated by this, but don't let it scare you! On the second day of creation God made the sky. "And God said, 'Let there be an expanse between the waters to separate water from water.' So God made the expanse and separated the water under the expanse from the water above it. And it was so. God called the expanse 'Sky' And there was evening, and there was morning – the second day" (Genesis 1:6-8).

The sky is a big deal, but it is meant to be wonderfully amazing, not overwhelming. Decorating can also be a big deal – it too is supposed to be incredibly fun and not overwhelming. I like to go into a room I am decorating and stare. I let whatever thoughts come to me, run through my mind. I picture all different sorts of activities that the room will inspire and picture a number of different colors floating around the space. One of the most important aspects of decorating for me is a prayer that pops out of my mouth almost involuntarily, "Lord, help me to make this room what it is supposed to be." Does decorating sound too unimportant to take to the throne of heaven? Does God care what color you paint your bathroom or which blinds you invest in for your home?

"The Lord said to Moses, 'Tell the Israelites to bring me an offering. These are the offerings you are to receive from them: gold, silver and bronze; blue, purple and scarlet yarn and fine linen; goat hair; ram skins dyed red and hides of sea cows; acacia wood; olive oil for the light; spices for the anointing oil and for the fragrant incense; and onyx stones and other gems'" (Exodus 25:1,3-7).

These directions for the Tabernacle were from the God of the Universe. He chose specific colors and materials and gave them to Moses to contract the work He wanted done in His Tabernacle. Sounds to me like a design job—with a decorator's draft board packed full of good ideas! In the Bible there is a story about some people building a tower. The Bible tells us God's response to their project, "But the Lord came down to see the city and the tower that the men were building" (Genesis 11:5). God came down to see their work. If God cared so much about His Tabernacle in the desert, and this God is the same yesterday and today and forever, then it stands to reason that He cares about design today and is excited about His creativity displayed in the work you will accomplish in your home. So don't forget to ask for His expertise in the planning of your space.

How We Perceive Color

You can go to school for years and still be perplexed by the magnitude of color. We must address the fact that our different personalities react differently to colors. It has been said that extroverts like red and orange. Introverts tend to be drawn toward blues and greens. As we grow, each of us develops likes and dislikes toward color based on experience, parental preference, intelligence, social class, and personality. Yellow is the fastest color seen and for this reason it is used for traffic warning signs. Purple is recognized as a "spiritual" color. It is also used as a sign of danger for atomic radiation. It is a common fact that more women like the color purple than men. Studies have shown that the darker color greens appeal to those of a higher social class.

Although I find these studies interesting, I want to be careful of placing too much credence in the findings made by fallible humans. God made our bodies and minds amazing and complex. It is no wonder that because of this, the simple matter of color is no longer simple. We seem to want a psychological reason for color. However, a fact simply remains: God made all of the colors and calls them all good. Balance is always the key. Just because your favorite color is red or green or blue, I would never suggest that you paint all the rooms in your house that one color. Color is not about just picking your favorite hue, because in truth your favorite color may be best offset with your least favorite color! We need to redefine the colors. Now the next exercise I want you to do may be more difficult for some than for others.

Some people are concrete learners. They tend to not be able to visualize as well as other personalities and this can be a hindrance to decorating decisions. However, once they have made up their minds, they stick to their decisions.

Some people are abstract learners. It will be easy for you to do this exercise.

Take out a box of crayons or close your eyes and remember colors. Children have little inhibition with color and like almost all the colors equally. Of course, you can have a favorite color, but let's balance our color feelings, and consider all the colors God made as *good*.

Think about your least favorite color. Why don't you like this color? Is it because your mom bought you that color dress for Easter one year and you wanted another? Is it because you ate corn and it made you sick so now you hate yellow? Do you not like a color because of how it looks on you? Did your grandma knit you one of those shawls (orange and olive green) and your mom made you wear it so you wouldn't hurt grandma's feelings? I am encouraging you to let all those past feelings about color go. Release your mind from color likes and dislikes for a few moments. Let's install some flexibility with the colors so that we can create a more balanced color palette for your home.

You sit staring at your white ceiling and walls with your tiny swatch of fabric and a few cards of paint chips trying to envision the entire room painted a certain color. Common questions arise:

1. How dark is too dark?
2. Where do I start and stop different colors?
3. If I paint the room a darker color will it make the room look smaller?

We want a simple answer to the questions above so that decorating remains fun and easy to do. So here goes:

1. How dark is too dark? Season to taste.
2. Where do I start and stop different colors? Wherever you want.
3. If I paint the room a darker color will it make it look smaller? Yes, but that is not always a bad thing.

With these answers being a little too simple, let's take a few minutes to explain.

You will drive yourself crazy if you follow the decision making method of "There is one best answer for this room and I am going to find it!" There is never just *one* answer for your room. There are a thousand different possibilities and each one of them can look fantastic.

Most people will choose several light colors, one or two medium tones and maybe one dark shade that appealed to them in the store, but they keep it in the "I would never paint my wall this color, but I sure do like it!" pile. Don't pass on painting with an

Ancient Egyptians painted using fresco style application and sealed it with a beeswax varnish.

extreme color simply because it scares you to paint it on your wall. Remember, we left fear in the waiting room. In order to answer some of these questions we need to learn what *the* Designer thinks about color.

The Designer's Thinking

On that first day of creation when God said, "Let there be light," He could have just as well said, "Let there be color," because light is color. When He created the sun – He created white light which has the ability to produce all colors. Everybody has a favorite color. God has given each of us instincts to put together a pleasing ensemble. After all, it is in His nature to create, and we were created in His image. We can learn a lot about what colors to use in decorating from the Creator of colors. Let's muse for a moment about what could possibly be God's favorite color. What value does He place on the different colors? This is the secret to unlocking our own knowledge of color for our homes.

COLOR BALANCE (HOW COLOR ACTUALLY IS) ACCORDING TO GOD

God is orderly and balanced in all that He does. He likes it when we do the same. "But everything should be done in a fitting and orderly way" (I Corinthians 14:40). Did God possibly use His favorite colors to paint the ceiling and walls of His favorite room? We have mentioned how He had Moses use purple, blue and red for the fabric of the Tabernacle. Four hundred and seventy six years later the Temple was built by King Solomon. The plans that Solomon carried out were given to him by his father King David who received them from God. "Then David gave his son Solomon the plans for the portico of the temple, its buildings, its storerooms, its upper parts, its inner rooms and the place of atonement. He gave him the plans of all that the Spirit had put in his

> "Send me, therefore, a man skilled to work in gold and silver, bronze and iron, and in purple, crimson and blue yarn, and experienced in the art of engraving . . ." II Chronicles 2:7

mind for the courts of the temple of the Lord and all the surrounding rooms, for the treasuries of the temple of God . . ." (I Chronicles 28:11,12).

So the color scheme for Solomon's Temple repeats the colors used in the wilderness for the Tabernacle more than four hundred years before. Purple, blue and red yarn were woven to make fabric.

The sun, which is made up of "white light," shines down on our atmosphere causing our sky to be painted certain colors. White light is made up of wavelengths of light, each wavelength of light gives a sensation of its own color. Just as the varying tightness of guitar strings changes notes, the different wavelengths of light produce different colors. One of the shortest wavelengths is blue – the shorter the wavelength the more that color is dispersed and scattered throughout the atmosphere. Therefore, the sky appears to be blue. However, a wavelength shorter than blue belongs to the color violet, but our not so perfect eyes cannot detect this color. Technically could we say the sky is purple? Now the next wavelength to pop up is red because it is the longest wavelength, putting it at the farthest end of the spectrum from blue. This is why, at times, we see a reddish cast in a sunset. Although all of the colors are represented in the sky – the three that predominate are blue, red and purple. So there we have it – God painted the ceiling and walls of His project with purple, blue and red, just as He used in the Tabernacle in the wilderness and just as He used in the Temple built by Solomon in B. C. 965. When someone uses the same colors many times, it is said that those are their favorite colors. There is a definite pattern in God's usage of these three particular colors. Any good decorator finds their niche and plans their project with what appeals to them and God started that process when He created the world. But although He distinctly uses three colors, He utilizes all of the colors in the creation of His world. In order to keep balance in decorating we will look at the entire color palette, but we will start with the basic question of:

WHAT APPEALS TO YOU? (HOW WE APPLY COLOR)

God made the spectrum of light and called it good. All the colors are good. What are your first three choices? Which colors are you drawn to first? There have been many studies on color and their effects on our moods. Some doctors suggest that our bodies respond either passively or aggressively toward color and one should be aware of using the "wrong" color in their home. Color, however, is not a moral issue. We have moral issues, but color is not one of them.

You may be thinking, *Well, I like all the colors, too, so how do I know what colors to chose?* This can be a huge dilemma for many people, causing them to run and look up the interior designer's phone number (not that that is a bad thing to do). But we are going to learn a method that will bring security to the mind of the indecisive.

QUESTION: HOW DO I KNOW WHAT COLORS TO USE IN MY ROOM?

There are many methods designers use for choosing colors. Colors have been chosen because of their symbolism, or because of their ability to change moods and set the atmosphere. Colors have been chosen, or cast aside because of people's inhibitions and fears. Elaine Ryan, author of "Color Your Life," has her clients go to the supermarket and pick out vegetables to see which colors appeal to them. Clients have had their walls repainted many times just to get the exact shade of taupe. Sometimes we pick colors based on how our best friend will react, or better yet, on how our mother will respond. Will she approve? We worry and fret about the "What ifs." What if I don't like the color, what if it is the wrong shade, what if my husband doesn't like the color, what if it doesn't match, or what if it goes out of style in the next couple of months? What if I get tired of it? How can we be sure to help you come out a winner when choosing a paint color? Good question!

In the Bible there are many references to color. Color has been used for centuries. Around 1400 B. C. they were able to dye garments and fabrics purple by using the tiny Muyex shell off the coast of Tyre. They did not yet have the knowledge of the spectrum of light that reveals colors, nor did they rely on the color wheel to ensure the correct usage of color for their garments or dwelling. They simply lived and used the colors that were available. They managed to live out their lives and create, not knowing the fundamentals of color. We can decorate without having completed the knowledge of color in its vastness because there is another sense that we will apply at this time. It is not one of the main five senses God granted us, but it is one we hopefully will apply and use for more than just decorating. A little thing called common sense plays a huge role in choosing color! Everyone has some common sense for color – use what you have.

> It took 336,000 snails to produce one ounce of dye.

Some people really love chocolate! I mean they really, *really* love chocolate! Other people like chocolate – it's nice to have, but they are not passionate about it. Should only people who love chocolate be allowed to eat it? With the different personalities God gave us, it is little wonder that we are drawn to different colors. You may be a person who likes to see some of the more passionate colors used in other people's homes. You may not be as passionate about the use of dark colors in your own home, but that does not mean you should not use a little. Just like chocolate – a little may go a long way for you. There is more balance in using a touch of a darker color than to not use any at all. May I also remind you that God says not

> Designer Thinking: Use your common sense!

to be anxious about anything (Philippians 4:6). Let's apply our common sense and see what happens to our color pallet!

The Closet:

Standing in my closet I am feeling in a bit of a rush. I have to be leaving for choir rehearsal in twenty minutes and I still don't know what I want to wear. I grab my red pants, and smile at my eight-year-old who is standing in the doorway.

"Do you want to come to rehearsal with me?"

"Oh yes!" she says enthusiastically.

By now I have chosen a short-sleeved black top and a camel colored vest with a touch of leopard print around the collar. My eight-year-old smiles and holds up my two tone purple and white zebra stripped neck scarf.

"Wear this Mommy!"

"Well, let's have a look." I take the scarf from her and tie it around my neck.

"What do you think?" I wait to see what the verdict is from the mind of a child.

"Oh, I like it!" she says smiling and I smile too. The mind of a child is not inhibited by colors and if they coordinate. This is refreshing and useful, but a little bit of training will go a long way. I begin to explain to her that there are three reasons why the scarf does not go with the ensemble:

1. The colors are not complimentary.
2. The patterns are not complimentary.
3. The styles are not complimentary.

The light began to turn on in her eight-year-old mind and she understood why I chose not to wear the scarf. It is basic common sense that most adults would have applied to the situation with no problem. They may not have thought about the three reasons, but they would have known that the scarf didn't complete the outfit. The same common sense that helps you get dressed in the morning can help you decorate your room, especially if you break it down into these three areas of color, pattern, and style. Many colors, patterns and styles are complimentary. Don't think you have to choose only one of each. It is fairly obvious when they do not belong together and I trust that you will know the difference.

So the long awaited answer to the question of "What colors do I choose?" is one of freedom!

- Choose the colors that appeal to you just like the Designer has done.
- Don't let fear rob you of color.
- Using balance, incorporate as many colors as you can.
- Use the common sense God gave you!

Extra tip when choosing colors:

Don't you hate it when you decide on a color and go shopping for accessories only to find that nobody else thought that color was great? All you wind up with is a bad mood and no accessories? Here is a tip. Before you make a final decision on a fabric with coordinating colors, take your swatch of fabric to the department store. Look at towels first, and then toothbrush holders, tissue boxes, sheets, pictures, and even plates. It doesn't matter what room you are intending the fabric to be used in – look at these items to clue you in on what designers are doing with color and what will be available to you in the near future. I stress near future, because you will not want to choose fabric and then pull it out of the closet ten years from now expecting to find matching accessories. In fact, I would not even put the project on hold for two years. If you are shopping and find a lot of clearance items with a great price - you better buy everything you want now, because it is on its way out. Out of the store that is, don't hesitate to go with a color that seems to be on "its way out" thinking it will not be in style. Colors can stay in style for years, you just want to make sure you are able to get the matching pieces you will need for your project while they are still in the stores. Happy hunting!

Design Homework:

In Chapter 1, you completed Jana's Decorating Personality Test. I find useful a system I call "Dial a Style." It is the key for reading the decorating test. It helps you to identify your stylistic preferences. I have grouped 12-15 different design styles into three basic, easy to understand styles. This will give you an idea of your overall goals in decorating and help you determine paint colors for your project. This is only a template, not the bible of choosing colors and style for your home. These styles correlate to the choices you made in Jana's Decorating Personality Test from Chapter 1.

If most of your answers were in the first column then you tend to lean toward the antique/classic side of decorating. If most of your answers were in the middle column then you tend to be in the trendy/eclectic side of design. If most of your answers were in the third or last column then you tend to be more modern in your approach to decorating. The cool thing about this system is that if you find yourself in a category you really don't want to be in, you can choose which one you would rather be in and simply change your style. It is a common misunderstanding that you have to "find" which style you are, as though you are born with a specific style and stuck in that category. Style is not a moral choice and you are not limited by your personality. Although it is true that your personality and preferences are often linked, if you decide that you want to try a different style than you have tried in the past, you can do that! Most people will find themselves in a couple of different categories – there are no wrong answers. This will help you see your tendencies and help you develop new decorating habits if that is your desire.

DIAL A STYLE

Style	Antique/classic	Trendy/eclectic	Modern/ contemporary/chic
Motivation in decorating	History Knowledge Comfort	Fun Color People Hospitality	Business Formality Change Clean lines
She Likes	What was in style	Her own style	What is in style NOW
Stores she likes to shop	Antique stores	Macy's or thrift stores	Target or Pier One
Number of paint colors	1–2	3	Extreme of 1–4
Colors they usually are drawn to	Creams Blues Greens Reds	White Gold Green Orange Brown	Black Red Purple Green

After going through your preferences using the decorating test and Dial A Style exercises, go to a paint or home improvement store and bring back no more than four color cards for reference. Don't worry about whether or not they go together, and don't try to picture how they will look on your walls or with your furniture – just pick the ones you like for now.

Spiritual Workshop and Spiritual Homework:

Let's talk a little further about this matter of shame. We are afraid of shame because we don't know how to handle ourselves when faced with it, and we fear the repercussions will be irreversible. Proverbs helps us understand where shame comes from. "When pride cometh, then cometh shame" (Proverbs 11:2 KJV). Fear and perfection are closely linked. Our desire to be perfect, and the fact that we never measure up to that expectation, frustrates our already paranoid view of fear.

We tend to be motivated by our desire for perfection – which plays a big role in our lives as women. It is our own endeavor to get back to the Garden of Eden. God made us to be perfect and it is little wonder that we long for it. We are all perfectionists in what matters to us, and we are all equally lazy at what does not motivate us, as long as no one is watching. Most of us believe the search for perfection is okay with God as there are many biblical references to doing your best and giving your best. But the doing and giving of our best is supposed to be for God. Most of the areas we spend perfecting are for ourselves. Psalm 39:5b says, "Verily every man at his best state is altogether vanity" (KJV). So the heart of perfectionism is not the desire to do one's best, as I had supposed, but the heart of perfection is selfishness. In our selfishness we have the attitude that only the best will do.

Along with perfectionism is presumption, for we presume we deserve perfection. Mark gives the account of the request of James and John. They asked for the privilege of sitting on either side of Jesus in eternity, which is presumptuous enough, but listen to the first verse of this passage. "Then James and John, the sons of Zebedee, came to him. 'Teacher,' they said, 'we want you to do for us whatever we ask'" (Mark 10:35-45). Not only were they asking to sit beside Him, but they preceded this request by saying they wanted Him to give them anything they wanted! What they wanted was not for His glory and honor, but for their own.

So selfishness and pride are the legs of perfection. Job voices his fears, "Even if I were innocent, my mouth would condemn me: if I were blameless, it would pronounce me guilty" (Job 9:20). We believe the lie of Satan that we deserve better than we are getting and God is not watching out for us. We let our minds condemn us with fear. The only counterbalance to fear and perfection is God's Word and God's love. "There is no fear in love. But perfect love drives out fear" (I John 4:18). When we focus on God's love – it drives out fear. I used to think perfection was something to reach for, but now I am putting perfection on the shelf and choosing God's love for me. I hope you will do the same.

A foundation for our spiritual walk is found in Matthew 19:26, "Jesus looked at them and said, 'With man this is impossible, but with God all things are possible.'" This is true in our spiritual lives and it can also apply to our desire to make our homes more pleasing. Take a couple of minutes to write out how this verse can apply to the area of interior design for your home and answer the following questions for your spiritual homework:

1. What keeps you from reaching the sky in your spiritual journey? Is there a sin that handicaps you? Yes or No
2. If a sin is still there because you have allowed it to stay, confess it as sin and move on.
3. Remember that fear of anything, except for God, is sin. What do you fear? Write it down and release it to God so that you can reach your full potential.
4. If you have confessed sin, don't allow Satan to keep you from the freedom that belongs to you. If you have

repented, God no longer holds that sin to your account. Psalm 103:12, "As far as the east is from the west, so far has he removed our transgressions from us."

The paint for your spiritual life is easy to define. It is simply God's Word. Without the Bible your spiritual walk is bland, just like without paint on our walls our earthly dwellings are without interest.

Incorporate spiritual needs into your life – reading the Bible and prayer. You wouldn't have a living room without a couch, or a dining room without a table. Equip yourself with God's Word and prayer for a truly inviting spiritual life.

A challenge for this week is to read from God's Word every day. Will you commit to taking this challenge?

Make yourself a promise and sign your name:

Chapter Three Recipe: Jana's Old World Wall Treatment

Do you want your room to have that warm old-world feeling at less cost then paying for all the fancy faux finishing paints you find in the hardware store? Then here is my own recipe for you to try. It is called "Erin's Room:"

Base coat: Behr gloss paint 360E-2 Castle Stone

Sponged top coat: Behr gloss paint 310F-4 Rye, and Behr gloss paint 340F-4 Expedition Khaki.

Glazed top coat: pour glaze into a container that a four-inch paint brush will fit into. For a touch of shimmer, add a 2oz bottle of metallic antique gold Folk Art acrylic paint. In another container squeeze, side by side, a dollop of artist's acrylic paint, colors—burnt sienna and burnt umber (found in most art stores). In a cross-hatch motion, wipe glaze on your wall with the four inch brush. Right away dip your brush into the container with the acrylic paint - dab the brush in both colors at the same time and with a stabbing motion apply the acrylic paint into the glaze on the wall. Keep pushing the paint using short stabbing motions to the upper right or left if you are left-handed. It will make the darker colors collect to resemble broken and painted over plaster. After you get the paint pushed around to your taste, take a piece of newspaper and put over the area you just painted. Rub your hands all over the newspaper then pull off. It will soften the lines of the faux finish. You can reuse the same piece of newspaper several times but it works best if you reuse it no more than five times. This type of painting will make your four inch brush only usable for this kind of painting so I suggest that you buy an inexpensive one to use.

If you want to add more interest you can try your hand at painting a crack on the wall. A nice accent color to use on another wall in the same room is: Behr gloss paint 150D-7 Regal red.

Psalm 69:32b-33a says, "You who seek God, may your hearts live. The Lord hears the needy."

Chapter 4

TOUCH OF MINK

(Creation Day Three)

*S*he staggers through the doorway, her clothes torn, her body *bruised but her spirit determined. She knows it must still be here, they took everything else and tried to get her to reveal its hiding place, but she had promised. Drained of energy her body forces her to the rough hewn planks of the floor. She drags her sweating, bleeding body across the splintered boards to the side of the hand-made mahogany bed. She gently caresses the sideboard; unlike the floor it is smooth and finished. She smiles sadly remembering her grandfather's perfectionist tendencies. Running her hand behind the board, her fingers trace the familiar knots in the grain serving as a map to hidden treasure. Just as the tip of her finger touches the submerged hinge she hears the weight of a foot on the stairs. The boards groan under the pressure and the "sh-sh" of a hand sliding up the iron banister causes her to immediately drop her hand and roll away from the bed. She grabs the side of the dresser and pulls herself upright. Taking the porcelain water pitcher from its place on the dresser she hobbles behind the door, poised and ready. She can* *feel the chip on the rim of the pitcher and the crack allows water to gently stream down her arms, offering unexpected refreshment.*

Designer's Workshop:

Can you feel the texture described in this scene? The word "texture" found in Merriam-Webster's Collegiate Dictionary is, "The identifying quality, the visual or tactile surface characteristics and appearance of something." Like adjectives used for clarification, so are the textures included in décor. When you look at an old trunk, for instance, your brain reminds you of what it would feel like to touch that object. In essence, texture to the decorator is when you can feel with your eyes. Texture is usually created by the combination of contrasts. For example: something old with something new, or something rough with something smooth. Contrast creates visual texture and is one of the main elements of design.

On the third day of creation God created dry ground and plant life (Genesis 1:9-13). At this point in history God created texture. Before the third day there had been only light and water. The addition of dry ground created not only land, but the feeling of texture. The difference visually between the smoothness of the water and the roughness of dry ground is enough contrast to make one stop and take notice, but then He adds to that duo a third party that completes the package. He adds foliage. Now we have the smoothness of the water, the roughness of dry ground and the beauty of the green shapely leaves of plant-life. This combination greatly stimulates the human brain. This is why so many of us rush off to some body of water for vacation and bask in the out of doors usually surrounded by these three elements – water, land and foliage - staring at them for hours. Hundreds of painters and photographers have given their life's work trying to capture the beauty of this particular combination.

In decorating, however, how do we know when and where to add this element of texture? I'm glad you asked![1]

My husband and I indulged in a weekend get-away to San Francisco. We stayed in a nice hotel. One morning I awoke a little early and my eyes came to rest on the "Do not disturb" sign hanging on the inside of our door. My mind raced to the possibility of a fire starting in a hotel and someone rushing up to knock on a door, but the door had the sign hanging on it, "Do not disturb." Does the person stop short and walk away saying, "Well, they don't want to be disturbed?" NO! Of course not! They would pound on the door anyway and warn them of the imminent danger.

Another time I was at a stop light in the middle lane of a six way stop. I look in my rear view mirror to see an ambulance with its lights flashing. Do I stay there because the light is red? Of course not! On earth we have protocol, but we also know when to break it. It's instinctive, it's practical, and its common sense.

In design the exceptions usually come because of just one reason. You must be ready with an answer to anyone who asks you, "Why did you do it like that?" I'm going to give you your answer before someone asks you that question. Here is your answer, "Because I like it that way!"

Often the scenario goes like this: "How do you like my design?" you ask as you point to an upside-down coffee cup gracing an end table.

"It goes the other way!" says the other person.

"Oh," you say as you put the coffee cup back to the same old position everyone else uses.

Let's see how using our design answer, "Because I like it that way," changes the outcome of this situation:

Coffee cup scenario take two – your friend sees the upside-down coffee cup sitting on the table and says, "Why is that cup upside-down?" You answer, "Because I like it that way!"

"But it goes the other way," presses the friend.

"Yes, but I want it this way – it's different." You say with a confident smile on your face.

The other person stops in their tracks, backs up, looks at the coffee cup and says, "Yes, marvelous, fantastic, I would have never thought of doing that, but how creative."

Design is supposed to do that! It is supposed to make you take notice and if you say it is supposed to be that way because of your desire for design, not only will others accept it, they

> Designer thinking: If everyone else does it one way, and you want to create a design element in a particular space, do it in a way no one would expect—think opposite.

will allow themselves to enjoy it for what it is – design! Design is supposed to make you breathe differently. This is why people will stand and stare at a red dot painted on a white canvas in awe. It's just a red dot! The painter decided one day to paint a red dot, and he did.

I can imagine some well-to-do art collector types hanging around the art gallery. One particular day they happen across the painting with the red dot. They say to each other, "What is so special about this painting." They know there must be something special about it or it wouldn't be hanging in *this* gallery. The owner of the gallery walks behind them and hears them musing. He looks up, "Oh, my goodness," He says to himself. "It is a red dot."

Out loud, wanting to sound like he knows what he is doing he says, "Yes, it is a red dot, but it is perfectly round!"

Oohs and aahs come from the couple who then go around the gallery and explain to everyone why it is so special. Before you know it there is a crowd gathered around singing the praises of the red dot.

I have a secret for you. It's not perfect! I know this because nothing under the sun is perfect! Deuteronomy 32:4, "He is a Rock, his works are perfect, and all his ways are just." God is perfect (II Sam. 22:31) and in Scripture when it speaks of being perfect, most of the time it is referring to the condition of our hearts. During the dedication speech given to the Israelites after bringing the ark into the temple, King Solomon says, "Let your heart therefore be perfect with the Lord our God, to walk in his statutes, and to keep his commandments . . ."(I Kings 8:61 KJV). We are to be perfecting our walk with Christ, but we spend much of our time trying to perfect things on earth that will never be perfect. Stop taking yourself out of the running for best designer because you can't seem to get it perfect. Designers don't have it perfect either; they just act like they do! I have never heard a designer say they made a mistake. Their answer is usually, "I meant to do it like that," or "I like it that way!"

Design is often about consistency followed by interruption. This is where our brains interpret texture. The interruption catches the eye forming the design. The unexpected is often more pleasing than the expected. This is the element of texture. The interesting thing about the sensation of touch is that each part of the body feels things differently. Touching a soft pillow with your big toe feels differently than touching the soft pillow with your hand or to your face. The brain God gave us remembers what it feels like to touch different kinds of objects. In perceiving texture, one of our eyes sees the object from one perspective creating a flat picture and our other eye sees the same object from another perspective creating another flat, or one dimensional picture. The image of the object is reflected to our retina which is also flat, but the brain puts them together and creates an area of dimension – then we can see texture.

God and texture

Water, land, water, land, land in the middle of the water, but it is still dry – texture. When the children of Israel crossed the Red Sea on dry ground with water walls to line the road they were surrounded by the awesomeness of the greatest Designer in the universe. The light of the pillar of fire provided a way for them to see and the softness of the light created atmosphere. The roughness of the dry ground in contrast with the smooth lines of the watery walls, enhanced by the pillar of light, must have been very stimulating to say the least.

How about the day Moses found the bush? He is walking along and sees a bush, bush, bush, bush on fire but not being burned up. Fire and leaves in the same place at the same time is surprising – that's texture!

Let's talk about the night Jesus was born. A King in a stable – that's a contrast! He was in a lonely stable probably made out of a cave. The ground covered with straw, the smell of animals in the air, the soft crying of a baby, the Shepherd visitors, and to top it off, the light from an angel enhances the moment. Can you almost smell those animals, and feel the straw beneath your shoes? Can you see the dust from the hay being shown through the light coming from the angel? And the baby, wrapped in cloths – and where did they lay him—in a hay-filled manger! That's texture. The contrast between the soft skin of a newborn and the hay surrounded by the wood of a manger – these all create texture!

Let's visit two more places in God's Word that create texture. Remember though, texture can be created by something you touch or by something that touches you. Atmosphere can be physically touching, emotionally touching, mentally touching, or spiritually touching. Let's think about the day Jesus died on the cross:

The King of Kings,
The old rugged cross,
The Son of God,
The crown of thorns pressing into His head,
The Prince of peace,
The nails piercing His flesh,
The Light of the World,
The darkness that veiled the Earth,
The Bread of Life,
The whip ripping the skin off His back,
The Lamb of God,
The sacrifice of God for me.

Another biblical example we will look at is Easter morning. The scene is this: three women, a big rock, an empty tomb, an angel in white garments sitting on the big rock, and a tomb surrounded by a beautiful garden. Death and life are being represented in the same place, "Why do you look for the living among the dead? He is not here; He has risen!" (Luke 24:5b-6a).

Texture can be created by what is imaginary or real, subtle or harsh. Texture is the adjective in decorating. It is descriptive enough to draw you into what is going on in the room. Texture can be made up of things that are useable or things that are not.

We stayed with friends for a couple of nights while we were en route to see relatives. Their house was a medium-sized house, not glamorous, not a dump – medium, but oh sooo comfortable! Beds for everyone, blankets and pillows softer than anywhere I've ever been! It was a great use of texture. Comfort texture–useable, practical texture.

We have some other friends – their house is full of texture, but you look at it, you don't touch it! It is beautiful and elegant, but you don't need to touch it to enjoy it. It is a different kind of enjoyment compared to the other house. Both are enjoyable for different reasons.

Texture and you

Similar to cultivating the palate, one needs to cultivate a more mature sense of design. Some are turned off by mixing or clashing patterns, mismatched woods, using unfinished or raw works, broken pottery pieces, and old things that are left weathered. Similar to the person who has acquired a taste for salad or coffee, cultivating your decorator's palate will give you confidence when you are in the marketplace for décor. It will help you sift through the myriad of available items, compiling a group of things that will represent you in your room. Hopefully, you have thought of some ways through the examples above of how you can incorporate texture in your own house. Here are a few more ideas to keep your creative mind going: flower pots, or any kind of pottery, garden gates, rocks, sand, bowls with water and floating candles, old tables, texture painted walls, iron sconces, or any unique object. Remember, texture is not about beautiful things, it is about creating beauty out of the things around you, some of which might be broken and ugly. Matthew 13:52 says, "Therefore, every scribe which is instructed unto the kingdom of heaven, is like unto a man that is an householder, which bringeth forth out of his treasure things new and old" (KJV).

Ancient Egyptians used mud from the Nile for plaster or brick for their homes. Sometimes they used stone for bathroom floors.

I have an affinity for ugly and broken items. I believe that the more weathered, beaten and broken the object is, the more it has to communicate, just by being itself. The beauty of something has very little to do with whether it is truly a beautiful item, but in the application of that item, incorporating other things around it. If you find that broken used item sitting in a dump surrounded by other hopeless items, it has little appeal. But when you bring that broken, used-up piece and set it in the midst of the beauty of your glass coffee table, it is transformed into an object of interest, making everything around it that much more beautiful.

Design Homework:

1. Write a sentence describing how you would like your room to feel – incorporate a scene with people responding and reacting in the space you are redecorating. Make sure to include a lot of adjectives.
2. After writing the sentence, on a separate piece of paper, write just the adjectives you used.
3. Take the list of adjectives you used and go shopping! Find at least one item that matches one of the adjectives on your list and put it in the room – notice if it adds the feeling you described in your paragraph.
4. Complete the choices made in the last two chapters and put them into action: Paint your room!

Spiritual Thinking:

Sometimes in order to create texture we have to be willing to get our hands dirty. How about the spiritual texture of our lives? In John 9 we find the story of Jesus healing a man who had been born blind. His disciples asked Him who had sinned, the man or his parents, that he should be born blind. Jesus answered that neither had sinned, but that God had allowed the man to be born blind so the work of God might be displayed in this blind man's life. Then Jesus spit on the ground, made mud, and put it on the man's eyes and healed him. Jesus could have whispered the command and healed him or just touched his eyes with clean hands, but He chose rather to get His hands dirty to heal the man.

Have we learned to say "no" too well? Under the quest to rebuild families, the admonishment to become less busy in order to accomplish a better home atmosphere went out a few years ago. As with all things, balance is the key. Of course we need to take care of our families! I wonder, however, if we are saying "no" to some ministry opportunities when God wants a "Yes" from us? "As long as it is day, we must do the work of him who sent me. Night is coming, when no one can work" (John 9:4). We who know Christ are the texture of the world, we are the contrast. "You are the salt of the earth. But if the salt loses its saltiness, how can it be made salty again?" (Matthew 5:13). We are to create the ambiance in the world, "You are the light of the world. A city on a hill cannot be hidden. Neither do people light a lamp and put it under a bowl. Instead they put it on its stand, and it gives light to everyone in the house. In the same way, let your light shine before men, that they may see your good deeds and praise your Father in heaven" (Matthew 5:14-16).

Philippians 2 says that we are to encourage, comfort, offer fellowship, and have tenderness and compassion for those around us. Remember, God is really really good with the broken, rough, dirty, and seemingly unwanted vessels. Don't overlook the people who can create the most texture in God's kingdom! God sees the beauty in the broken. There was a woman with a blood disease he healed in Luke 8:43-48. Mark 14:3-9 describes a woman who broke her jar of perfume and poured it on Jesus' head. Jesus saw the beauty in the life of this woman with the broken jar.

I believe we have misunderstood God's desire for our lives. We are obsessed with being perfect as we touched on earlier. We think God is looking for perfection when all He wanted to do was provide it for us. God wants us to perfect our humility and brokenness before Him. He likes broken, he can work with broken. He has very little use for perfect. King David says in Psalm 51:16,17, "You do not delight in sacrifice, or I would bring it; you do not take pleasure in burnt offerings. The sacrifices of God are a broken spirit; a broken and contrite heart, O God, you will not despise."

Jesus picked Mary sitting at His feet over Martha's desire to put on a perfect meal. God picked the widow's coin over the wealthier offering. And God picked the man who beat his chest in grief crying out "God be merciful to me a sinner" over the man who prayed piously on the corner. So we need to be broken before God, but how do we do that? The fact is, we are already broken—we just have to admit it! This is where that humility God loves so much comes into use. His perfect love separates us from fear.

Last of all, maybe you're a person who feels like you're the "broken" vessel. Maybe your thought is, *I'm not striving for perfection – It's all I can do just to get up in the morning!* Maybe you've gone through a divorce and you can't seem to feel like a whole person again. Maybe you've lost a loved one and it has left a void in your life you just can't get over. Isaiah 61:1-3, "He has sent me to bind up the brokenhearted, to proclaim freedom for the captives and release from darkness for the prisoners, to proclaim the year of the Lord's favor. . ."

Don't forget, God is really, really good with broken things! If you find yourself fitting into this category, God wants to decorate His world with you. You add that spice of life He can really use. Be encouraged and remember, *Save Perfection for Heaven* – God is.

CHAPTER FOUR RECIPE: SETTING A "SAVE PERFECTION FOR HEAVEN" HOLIDAY TABLE

One of my favorite ways to add texture to my home during the holidays is by setting an extraordinary fun - breath-taking table.

- **Candle Holders:** clean soup cans make nice center pieces when you spray-paint them an appropriate color. I usually use silver or gold—something metallic, and yes, I realize that they are already silver, but they look nicer when you paint them. You can put candles in them and let them stand alone, or you can take three of them and tie them together with raffia or ribbons. They work best as candle holders when you put sand or tissue paper in the bottom of them to have something to push the end of the candles into.

    Another item I enjoy using as candle holders for the table are different sizes of Mason Jars. I use sand in the bottom and a very long white taper candle that I push into the sand. Sometimes I take a few sea shells, broken colored glass or marbles and sprinkle or place around the candle on top of the sand. Using several of these down the middle of the table is very elegant. I like to have several things going down the center of the table. These usually include the following in some form: candles, flowers or greenery, garland or garnish of some kind. And I like to provide different levels by either putting pillars of some kind underneath the items or by hanging lighter items using fishing wire and a white thumb tack to push into the ceiling. Example: one time I bought three rust colored wrought-iron votive hanging candle holders meant to be used outside - these were great to hang from the ceiling and I hung them at different heights.

- **Table Accessories:** Shells are also interesting to use on your holiday table. Put a medium/large shell by each place setting. Serve salad dressing in these cleaned out shells. Or melt candle wax in shells and don't forget to install a short wick. These make nice little candles—put several of them down the center of the table.

    1. **Placemats:** Make placemats using a technique you learned in grade school. Use brown paper that is sometimes used for mailing packages. Cut ovals that are larger than your dinner plates. Then light the edge of the paper ovals with a match. Let burn slightly and then blow or snuff out. Create a burned edge all around the placemats. You can do several at one time if you stack them. I would suggest doing this activity outside or in the garage. These add a lot of texture to the table. And when you put them with dishes and table linens it creates a great contrast.

    2. **Table Center:** At Christmas time I like to put Christmas lights down the center of the table—sometimes wrapped around garland.

    3. **Nut Cups:** Other nice additions to a holiday table are little clay pots that I put nuts or candies into. You can keep them clay colored or paint them metallic silver or black for a bit of elegance.

    4. **Napkin rings:** Use wire found in most hardware stores. Twist into napkin holders using any shape you want. Leave an extra curl or two that can be used to hold name cards.

    5. **Tablecloths:** one easy way to make an inexpensive table covering is to go to the fabric store.

Save Perfection For Heaven

There are many types of fabric that don't need to be hemmed and even if you choose one that does, you can tuck under the unfinished edges. It is also very effective to buy one long piece for the underneath layer—then buy a couple of extra yards of coordinating fabric to make into two squares and put at an angle on top of the first layer. You will have a very custom looking table at a very friendly price.

6. **Accessories:** Garden items are nice to use on the table.

Psalm 74:16-17 says this about God, "The day is yours, and yours also the night; you established the sun and the moon. It was you who set all the boundaries of the earth; you made both summer and winter."

Chapter 5

HEARING IS UNDERSTANDING

(Creation Day Four)

THE BUSY SUMMER COTTAGE

Our friends have automobiles now. The summer cottage
  where we went
To rest beside the water's blue in peace and indolent content
Is but an hour's swift ride away. So bright and early Sunday
  morn
Before the breakfast eggs are cooked, we hear the honking
  of the horn.
We must have bathing suits for ten, although our family
  numbers four;
Beds must be made for all who come, though father sleeps
  upon the floor;
Dishes and knives and forks and spoons are gathered in one
  huge display,
For we must be prepared to feed the visitors that come our
  way.

91

From Friday noon till Monday morn full many a wary trip
    I take
Rowing the women and their babes upon the bosom of the
    lake;
And by the law which rules a host I'm at the mercy of the
    crew,
I must, until they say good-bye, do everything they wish I
    do.
The chef in yonder large hotel is not a busier man than I,
The fish for fifteen hungry mouths it is my duty now to
    fry,
And thus my glad vacation time from dawn to dusk is filled
    with chores,
For friends have made our resting spot the busiest place in
    all outdoors.

By Edgar A. Guest

Designer's Workshop:

When we consider the sense of hearing in regard to decorating, we must venture into another avenue of our lives that marries decorating to hospitality. Of all the things we were meant to be as humans, one of them is hospitable, even if it is just to our neighbor who needs to borrow our lawn chairs. Hospitality sounds like doorbells ringing, dishwashers washing, voices calling, telephones ringing, laughter, piano keys being played, computers, television, game-boys, birds chirping, grandfather clocks ticking, traffic passing, and children's voices echoing through the hallways.

Basically, hospitality is loud, but fun. I hope we never get tired of being interrupted by having other people in our lives. When you let people into your life, they will wear you out, use all your soap and toilet paper, call you at all hours, ask you to watch their children overnight, help themselves to the food in your refrigerator, come in without knocking and bring the neighborhood with them. If other people feel comfortable helping themselves to a glass of water in your house without asking, congratulations, you are hospitable! If you struggle allowing people that much access to your life – lighten up, enjoy life, and invite others to enjoy it with you. I'm going to ask you to file this little bit about hospitality away because we are going to revisit the subject when we talk about the sensation of taste.

As we consider the sensation of hearing in this area of decorating it seems to play an insignificant part. However, imagine a scary movie without the sound effects that make you jump out of your seat, or a circus without the appropriate music. Imagine a ball game without the horn announcing the quarters and without the sound of the ball bouncing on the wood floor of the gym while the crowd cheers and makes other crowd-like noises in the background. All of these subtle things in life can make a difference. Many of these things are just part of the package, but someone *planned* them at one time. My goal for you in this chapter is to *plan* the sounds that will make up the atmosphere of your home.

When there is noise, we quite often refer to it as "commotion," the root word being "motion." The significance of this is the fact that our ears allow us to sense motion. So the sensation of hearing is also the sensation of motion – an awareness of what is going on around us. The human ear has a special sense known as "Angular Motion." This happens because we have three canals in each ear enabling us to sense motion three-dimensionally. Just as the eye gives us three dimensional vision, the ear gives us three dimensional hearing. This is why a loud noise can make us jump – it gives us the sensation that something is after us, or something is falling. A mother hears a loud noise coming from her toddler's room and she runs up the stairs – why? Because she senses that there was a motion that might have been harmful to her child. This is why we respond with compassion to the sound of a child softly crying. These sensations hit our ears first and then our brains respond to the stimulation. So what stimulation do you want present in your home? What atmosphere do you want to purposefully create?

"Hi Honey, how was your day at work," Missy asks as she cradles the receiver on one shoulder, stirs the boiling pasta with one hand and kisses her husband who just came in the door.

(To Sue on the phone) "Sue, I should let you go, I've got to finish supper, you know how it is!"

"Peter, stop hitting your sister and go wash up for supper." Missy starts setting the table and grimaces as she hears the door-bell. "Honey, would you answer the door please? I just don't know who it could be."

The husband answers the door and the smiling salesman asks, "Would you have a few moments to witness the awesome power of the most powerful vacuum on the market?"

"Well," the husband pauses looking back into his haven of chaos. "I don't see why not! Come on in."

"Sally, stop jumping on the couch," says the wife as she joins her husband at the front door.

"Honey, who is this? Supper is almost ready and, Peter, I said stop hitting your sister!" she looks at her husband for an explanation of the stranger in her home, wondering if he is a dinner guest she forgot she invited. She stands there with oven mitts on her hands and a scowl on her face directed at her children who are still arguing. Mentally she is trying to count the meat and potatoes for her family and this man who must be joining them for dinner, but why does he have a vacuum with him? Just then, the phone rings!

How many of us have been in this scene! I am pretty sure I was in it last night. It's not a great place to come home to if you're a man and certainly doesn't do a lot to boost the self-esteem in us women! So, what can we do to make sure our home feels inviting? Obviously in this woman's case, some of the dilemma is the discipline of her children! Now, that's a different book altogether, but definitely worth checking into when you are trying to purposefully create a pleasant atmosphere in your home. The discipline factor aside – most of the problems in this scene could have been solved by planning ahead! Planning has as much to do with creating good atmosphere at home as it did when you planned your wedding. Did your wedding go off without a hitch? Probably not, but can you imagine if you had done no planning at all? Planning a family meal like you would plan a wedding reception may seem a bit drastic, but aren't we really talking about changing our habits? If we are in the habit of throwing something together at the last minute while hubby is coming through the door, and we are finishing up the conversation with Sue on the phone, while we have given our children no prior direction, the inevitable ensues and all of a sudden we are playing out the scenario above. It's not just dinner time drama that can steal our atmosphere. What about our phone voice when our spouse calls from work at a less than convenient time?

"Hello! Yes, well I can't help that right now – I told you! I've got to get the girls to gymnastics and the dog to the vet. I gotta go – I told you these things, why can't you remember them?"

O.K., maybe it's not always directed at your spouse: "Sarah, I told you to pick up your toys, I've got company coming over any minute – now scoot!"

When we plan ahead it usually takes the bite out of our suppertime attitude. But there is another aspect of home life that keeps us on edge in our decorating world.

Beware of prohibitive decorating

All the noise of a busy household sometimes inhibits us from decorating. We think it will be easier once the kids are older or leave the house. Sometimes people will go ahead and decorate and then allow no one to enter the room. Both of these thoughts are prohibitive as it either prohibits people from decorating, or it prohibits family (kids) or friends (friend's kids) from being able to be themselves. So decorate, but keep balance in mind.

Life seems to be made up of one big distraction, separated temporarily by moments of real life. Somewhere between the moment you find your child writing with permanent marker on the wallpaper and your reaction, is that split second when you see real life. You may even see the humor in it, but it is quickly snuffed out by the adult realization that you're mad because a permanent marker is permanent! Once in a while I am able to hold on to that second and actually respond correctly. These are the times I feel like I experience real life. A lot of people live such busy lives they don't actually live. I know this because sometimes that person is me. Sometimes I am so busy getting everything done that at the end of the day when I am tucking my kids into bed, I suddenly realize I haven't seen them all day. A moment's glance up from doing the dishes doesn't really count. What really counts? When we start *thinking* about living, instead of just living, almost everything becomes enjoyable – even opportunities to discipline.

> Don't let perfectionism rob you of life.

You find little Johnny painting the walls with pudding. The old thinking would say, "Great, now I have to get everything clean and new and perfect looking," which leads to anger and unhappiness. New thinking causes us to step back, watch, and remember. It allows us to let it soak into our memory. One or two more strokes of pudding won't make it any worse than it is. Remember, someday Johnny will be thirty instead of three – he may be a doctor, or in this case, an artist. Enjoy the moment, and then enjoy the opportunity Johnny has given you to discipline him and help him to become what Jesus wants. The old thinking comes from that perfectionist's thinking that everything must be perfect. Don't let perfectionism rob you of life.

Creating nostalgia by way of sound

When you are purposefully creating an atmosphere for a specific occasion, one thing to include is a song that brings back memories. It could be music that you listened to on your first date or a song that was played at your wedding. For Valentine's Day one year, my husband put some love songs on a CD for me. I listened to the music while I decorated for the Valentine's dinner I was preparing for five other couples. Do you think I was in the right frame of mind by the time my guests arrived? Yes, I was!

Adding the right music at the right time is like having your walls painted a great color. Music is the paint for parties. No wonder God chose to have angels show up at the birth of Christ saying – Glory to God in the highest! How many times have we sung that phrase at Christmastime? Can you imagine the Christmas story without the music? During most important occasions there will be something about the music that brings precious memories to mind. So instead of just leaving it to chance, plan your music to create special memories. I guarantee it will be just as enjoyable. Believe it or not, spontaneity usually has to be planned.

Design homework:

Let me be the first to say that I have not mastered or even come close to creating the kind of atmosphere I really want to be present in my home! It is a constant conviction and something I am working on – but what a difference when I plan wonderful sounds that promote rest, playfulness, thoughtfulness, and refreshment! When taking the time to plan ahead, here are some things to consider:

1. Start before you think you need to – if supper is at 6:00, start at 4:30. (Planning when to have supper also helps!)
2. Take inventory of what you need at the beginning of the day. Then, if you are missing something, you will have time to get it.
3. Have the kids clean up while you start supper. Tell them you want everything to look great when Dad comes home. For those whose husbands travel or for those raising kids on their own, just tell them you want a nice family dinner and you need their help. If they get done straightening and putting toys away, have them help you with simple age-appropriate items. Setting the table is fairly easy even for very young people.
4. Turn off the T.V., put on some music, light a candle, and ignore the phone. What a difference it makes when I do this! There are many times during the day when these principles could be applied.

Keeping the creating of atmosphere in mind, let's move forward to see what God made on day four of creation.

As different as night and day

"And God said, 'Let there be lights in the expanse of the sky to separate the day from the night, and let them serve as signs to mark seasons and days and years, and let them be lights in the expanse of the sky to give light on the earth'" (Gen. 1:14-15).

On the fourth day, God created not just the sun, moon, and stars, but He also created the seasons! As humans we may decorate *for* the seasons, but God decorates *with* the seasons using them as a tangible attitude changer. We have been talking about the sense of hearing and how sounds create different atmospheres. God created different atmospheres by giving us our sense of hearing. He also created changing atmospheres with the changing of the seasons. That is why, for some reason, Christmas seems more "Christmasy" when there is snow on the ground, or preferably falling gently from the sky. It does not seem "Christmasy" if there is a blizzard that leaves snow drifts up past the doorway. In creation we can see at least four types of atmospheres God created.

> Designer's Thinking: seasons are the backdrop of life.

1. Fun atmosphere
2. Romantic atmosphere
3. Orderly atmosphere
4. Spiritual atmosphere

Summer is thought of as the fun season. The sun shining on a sandy beach or in the back yard by the pool are reflections of what summer fun is in our mind's eye—long days with nothing pressing to be done and lemonade in tall glasses complete the picture. Then there is autumn – I think fall is somewhat interchangeable with winter, the Christmas season. Both of these can be romantic and spiritual. Fall is a time to reflect, to cozy in for the upcoming winter. The smell of burning leaves and cool wind remind you snow is just around the corner. It is a time to walk hand in hand and enjoy the season together.

Winter can be very romantic with Christmas, snow, and holiday feelings in the air. Sleigh rides and mistletoe contribute to the aura of romance, but the facts of Christmas bring us to the spiritual side to celebrate Jesus' birthday! My husband also recalls that snow in the wintertime makes everything quieter. My friend Deb mentioned the sound of the snow crunching under our feet as a distinct wintertime memory.

Now we come to spring. Winter is finally over – time to clean. Spring is definitely an orderly season. Getting kids ready for summer vacation, cleaning out closets, washing windows, and getting the camper ready for family trips are all part of spring. The snow melts away and new life is forming all across the country. Spring is a time for order and new life. These were all designed by God on the fourth day of creation. God uses these four atmospheres in the seasons. There are also biblical examples of His use of the elements of nature in His relationship with mankind.

In one of God's meetings with Moses on Mount Sinai, God descended upon the mountain in fire, consuming the mountain in smoke. Then came an earthquake that shook the whole mountain, followed by the sound of a trumpet that kept getting louder. When Moses spoke to God, God answered him with thunder. Talk about creating atmosphere! Now, there's a Designer who knows how to make an entrance!

In the book of I Kings we find the story of Elijah, a prophet of God. He had been doing the Lord's work, but it didn't seem to be going the way the prophet thought it should – so he hid in a cave. God finds him in this cave and says,

> "Go forth and stand on the mountain before the Lord." And behold, the Lord was passing by! And a great and strong wind was rending the mountains and breaking in pieces the rocks before the Lord; but the Lord was not in the wind. And after the wind an earthquake, but the Lord was not in the earthquake. And after the earthquake a fire, but the Lord was not in the fire; and after the fire a sound of a gentle blowing. When Elijah heard it, he wrapped his face in his mantle and went out and stood in the entrance of the cave. And behold,

a voice came to him and said, "What are you doing here, Elijah?" (I Kings 19:11-13)

In this story from God's Word, we see God using atmosphere to drive home a point! I can guarantee that God had Elijah's attention.

In the book of Matthew, Jesus was busy teaching people and the day became long. People were hungry. He had the disciples see if anyone brought food with them. A boy had a small lunch – two fish and five loaves of bread and Jesus had everyone sit down. A good host or hostesses knows how to guide their guests. When everyone was seated, Jesus blessed the bread and began dividing it for the people. He provided for everyone and had food to spare (Matthew 14:13-21). A good host will have enough for everyone, better too much than not enough. A good host will also be creative. For instance, if you find you have more guests than you anticipated, it might be more worth your while to cut portions smaller than to run to the store. Jesus created an orderly atmosphere.

Plan purposefully to make these four atmospheres of life happen for your family and guests. When you endeavor to create these atmospheres in your home, you go a step further than most people. It makes a noticeable difference. It may have very little to do with what people typically think of as "decorating." You may not change the paint, or carpet, but if you insert the elements of atmosphere, people will think that you did something truly amazing!

More Design Homework:

1. Think of the space you are decorating. Decide what kind of atmosphere you are creating in relation to the four types of atmospheres described in this chapter:

1. Fun atmosphere
2. Romantic atmosphere
3. Orderly atmosphere
4. Spiritual atmosphere

2. You will probably want to choose two of the four types of atmospheres to be present in your room – a first place and a second place. Keep in mind that you will use all of these throughout your home, so don't feel like you have to make each of them appear in each room.

3. Make a list of sounds you enjoy hearing and a list of sounds that annoy you. Plan how to emphasize the sounds you desire in your space.

Example: While I was growing up, my mother played old music and talked about how her mother listened to that same music when she was growing up. I found a record player in my grandmother's basement and held on to it. I collect old records and play them for my children. I explain to them that my mother and grandmother listened to this type of music and we laugh and have fun with how different the music sounds compared to today's music. I even give them quizzes to see if they can guess if it is Dean Martin or Nat King Cole singing.

Spiritual Thinking:

James 1:22 says, "But be ye doers of the word, and not hearers only..." (KJV).

The thing about hearing is that it should always lead to doing! The activities that are heard in your home should be motivational in some direction. Hearing children laughing and playing should lead to smiling if nothing else. Music often leads to dancing. Good news leads to rejoicing. Loud noise leads to covering your ears. Words of affirmation lead to confidence which leads to better workmanship. So let me ask you, what is keeping you from being what God wants you to be? Are you really obeying God in every area – including the area of being hospitable? Basic obedience means God is at home within the areas of your life. What area needs to be cleaned out in your life so that God, who is holy, feels comfortable?

People who are open-minded to what they are hearing are positive persons who will actually do something with what they have learned. A person who has a hard time remaining flexible to all possibilities may have a harder time connecting with a creative or spiritual idea. So be like the book of James encourages us – be a doer and not just a hearer. You will be much more satisfied with the results!

Spiritual Homework:

The following verses are about God's power and creation and sound. After looking up the verses below, write down some interesting things you learn about God and His creation of sound. They may inspire your decorating project.

Psalm 77:13-20
Psalm 98
Psalm 150

CHAPTER FIVE RECIPE: HOW TO INSPIRE YOUR CHILDREN TO ENJOY A PEACEFUL ATMOSPHERE

Are you having one of those days where the kids seem to be bouncing off the walls? Try this recipe for creating a tolerable atmosphere – without removing the kids, turn off the lights in the house and light a few candles. Turn on some soft soothing music and have the kids sit on the couch. Tell them you are going to have a quiet day and that they can pick a book that you will read, but that they are going to have to listen carefully because you are going to read it in a quiet voice because it is a "quiet" day. See if this doesn't change your chaotic day into a rather nice one.

Psalm 45:7-8 says "You love righteousness and hate wickedness; therefore God, your God, has set you above your companions by anointing you with the oil of joy. All your robes are fragrant with myrrh and aloes and cassia. . ."

Chapter 6

SMELLING IS TELLING

(Creation Day Five)

On the fifth day of creation God created everything in the sea and in the air. Water and air are two essentials we need to survive! On day five, God filled these two main essentials with interest – He decorated our survival kit. Before He created giraffes, elephants, cows, pigs or horses, He made everything that swims or lives in water and every animal that fills the sky. In decorating it is important to remember this example He gives us, because it works so much better when we finish everything around the room before we fill up the mainland with its occupants – even though they may be more familiar to us – like couches, chairs, and end-tables.

Designer's Workshop:

In the grand scheme of things, noses are not easily overlooked! It is one of the first things people want to change about their physical appearance, and just think of the number of products created just to please this sensitive area of our bodies. At any number of stores we can pick up gum, perfume, body lotion, deodorant, room spray, plug-ins, incense, potpourri, candles, drop-ins for the toilet, kitty-litter with fragrance pellets, aroma therapy, not to mention diaper genies, Altoids, and Febreeze! In fact, whole stores have been invented just for the pleasure of our smellers. We no longer want Windex that smells like Windex, but Windex that smells like flowers. We want our laundry to have the fragrance of the open field even though we pulled it out of the dryer. The clean smell isn't enough anymore, now we want our bleach to smell like the country or a rose garden. We don't want our kitties and doggies to smell like animals, our homes to smell lived in, our bathrooms to smell like we use them, our kids to smell like they have been playing, our husbands to smell like they've been mowing the grass, our car to smell less than new or our refrigerator to smell like food. The fragrance industry is booming. We have given them a run for our money – and we willingly pay the price to keep this small member of our bodies very, very happy! Why is this do you suppose?

Our sense of smell comes from a membrane called the olfactory epithelium. This olfactory tract is part of the brain that makes up the limbic system which includes emotional behavior and memory. It should come

> Designer Thinking: fragrance is part of decorating.

as no surprise to us that our senses of smell and taste are linked, and in addition to these, our behavior and memory systems react. All four of these make up a strange kind of "blended family" which plays a huge role in our everyday life. Not only are humans able to distinguish up to 10,000 different smells, but these odors are transmitted to our brains using neurons carrying an electrical signal. This is very complex for something that usually affects my everyday life with something like "I think I need to change a diaper!" It seems to me that, given all this information, the whole smelling sensation takes on a more important role than one would think. Let's see how it affects the decorating of our homes.

It is known that smells evoke memories – good or bad. A mother knows the smell of her baby. I love the smell of crayons and school supplies. The smell of rain in the air makes me want to start baking bread (using a bread-maker of course!). And how many times has someone said that your house has a distinct fragrance? Do you remember the fragrance of your grandmother's house? I do. My grandma's house smelled of cooked cabbage and moth balls. Believe it or not, it is a good memory for me! My other grandma's house smelled of Salem Lights, but only slightly because she smoked in the bathroom, never in front of us. We could talk all day about the memories that come from smelling certain odors, but what can we do about some of the odors we want to change?

One designer solution to a fragrant home is to fill baggies with potpourri. Make holes in the bags for ventilation and put these sachets in the air vents throughout the house. I have seen a more professional version of these sold in some home improvement stores. Candles are always nice, even in the summer! Some candles are so fragrant that you do not even need to burn them to enjoy their fragrance! It stands to reason that garbage is a good thing not to keep in the house. I have learned the hard way to take the garbage out of the house as often as possible! The more often you take the garbage out the less of a chance of odor lingering. There are also spray fresheners for garbage cans that will help take care of the problem. Let's consider a more introspective part of what we breathe in spiritually.

In Exodus 30:34-38 God gives a recipe for incense to be used only for Him. The incense was made from gum resin, onycha, galbanum, and pure frankincense. It was to be salted and pure. It was so important to God that this fragrance be kept only for Him, that verse 38 says, "Whoever makes any like it to enjoy its fragrance must be cut off from his people."

> As with all good designers - God has His own fragrance

Incense in the Bible is used for prayer. When incense was burned it was at the same time that prayers were offered. David says in Psalm 141:2, "May my prayer be set before you like incense." I take this to mean that good conversation and good fragrances go hand in hand. At least, God thinks this to be the case. We could keep this in mind when we plan a family night. Sometimes we only think of lighting candles when we have loaned the kids out for the evening, but they will enjoy the atmosphere of candlelight as well. How homey it feels when we heat up a dessert – like cherry pie or cinnamon rolls! These are conversation starters all by themselves. Having the windows open to let in the fresh spring air is another fragrance to enjoy. There are so many things we can add to the feeling of our homes when we include fragrance on our shopping list.

Design Homework:

1. Begin using the ideas you have recorded.
2. Start a journal of ways to encourage guests. Keep it in the room where you do most of your entertaining. Don't be afraid to ask people what you can do to meet their needs.

What Fragrances does God Like?

The book of Genesis shares a time when God decided to start over! Even the best designers decide to start over at times. The account of Noah is a good example of this:

> The Lord saw how great man's wickedness on the earth had become, and that every inclination of the thoughts of his heart was only evil all the time. The Lord was grieved that he had made man on the earth, and his heart was filled with pain.

> So the Lord said, "I will wipe mankind, whom I have created, from the face of the earth—men and animals, and creatures that move along the ground, and birds of the air—for I am grieved that I have made them." But Noah found favor in the eyes of the Lord (Gen. 6:7-8).

So God started over. He flooded the whole earth with water and only Noah and his wife, with their three sons and their wives were saved. God used eight people to start the creation project anew. God, the Architect, gave Noah specific instructions to build a boat and God told Noah He was going to establish a covenant with him. The Bible goes on to say that Noah did everything God told him to do. Then the water came, and came and came – for forty days and nights until only those on the ark remained. The waters stayed on the earth for a hundred and fifty days. After the waters receded and the ark came to rest on the top of a mountain, God called to Noah, "Come out of the ark, you and your wife and your sons and their wives. Bring out every kind of living creature that is with you – the birds, the animals, and all the creatures that move along the ground – so they can multiply on the earth and be fruitful and increase in number upon it" (Gen. 8:16-17). God chose to utilize some of the product of His first creation to finish His project. He didn't throw it all away.

After Noah and his family came out of the ark they celebrated by offering sacrifices to God.

> Then Noah built an altar to the Lord and, taking some of all the clean animals and clean birds, he sacrificed burnt offerings on it. The Lord smelled the pleasing aroma and said in his heart; "Never again will I curse the ground because of man, even though every inclination of his heart is evil from childhood. And never a gain will I destroy all living creatures, as I have done. As long as the earth endures, seedtime and harvest, cold and heat, summer and winter, day and night will never cease" (Genesis 8:20-22).

Their response pleased God – it smelled good to Him. It was the fragrance of obedience. When they got off the boat – and finally out of their trial – they did not have the attitude that focused on their problems. They could have said, "Well, finally – it's about time we got out of here, God really owes us for making us stay in here all this time." They focused on God instead of themselves. God was so pleased with Noah's response, that He made a covenant with Noah that is passed down to all mankind.

> I establish my covenant with you; Never again will all life be cut off by the waters of a flood; never again will there be a flood to destroy the earth. And God said, "This is the sign of the covenant I am making between me and you and every living creature with you, a covenant for all generations to come: I have set my rainbow in the cloud, and it will be the sign of the covenant between me and the earth. Whenever I bring clouds over the earth and the rainbow appears in the clouds, I will remember my covenant between me and you and all living creatures of every kind" (Gen. 9:11-15a).

You will notice God did not say – When you see the rainbow you will remember my promise, but God says, "When *I* see the rainbow, *I* will remember *my* covenant!" The next time you see a rainbow, realize that God is remembering His promise to you! What I find interesting from a design standpoint, is that God used the color spectrum in a more vis-

A rainbow forms when sunlight hits the top of raindrops and is refracted through each drop of rain and reflects through the bottom of each drop. You get a different view of the same rainbow depending on where you are standing. For this reason, everybody sees his very own rainbow, even if a hundred people are staring at the same rainbow.

ible form to us as a symbol and to Himself as a reminder. This part of history exhibits the personal relationship God desires to have with us.

Spiritual Thinking:

Providing the essentials for others who either live in your environment or for those who are just visiting is important. If basic essentials for living are water and air, then a basic essential for spiritual living is to make sure that the people around you have what *they* need to grow. Here are three guidelines I use to exhort myself in keeping with God's essentials:

1. Always remember
2. Always refresh
3. Always reflect

Always Remember:

God makes a point of remembering special dates or times and encourages us to do the same. Remember the story about Joshua building an altar for a memorial with the stones from the Jordan River – it was God's idea!

God also encourages symbols to help us remember to obey! In Numbers the Lord told Moses to have the Israelites wear a blue tassel on their garments. When they looked at the tassel they would remember the laws of the Lord and obey.

Always Refresh:

Paul says in I Corinthians 16:18, "For they refreshed my spirit and yours also. Such men deserve recognition." Paul says again in II Timothy 1:16, "May the Lord show mercy to the household of Onesiphorus, because he often refreshed me and was not ashamed of my chains."

Paul spoke continually of those who "refreshed" him. Are you refreshing to be around? Are you a humidifier or a dehumidifier? All of us have been around those who "fill" us up, encourage us, and send us on our way ready to conquer the world. And all of us have been around those who suck the life right out of us. When we leave them we feel depressed and search to find significance in life.

Are you room darkening blinds, keeping the room from one ray of light, or are you like sheers letting the "Son" shine through you to make others smile? Are you a bathroom scale being truthful even though it may hurt a bit, or are you a blender ignoring the good and the bad – pureeing them into a shallow consistency? Are you a VCR keeping records of all things good and bad ready to play them back at a moment's notice? Are you a crock-pot or a microwave? Do you sit and stew or get it done and move on with life? Are you a warm blanket or a wet blanket? You might say, "Well, I'm not that bad. I'm not that kind of woman." What kind of woman are you? Remember I said I was going to ask you – and the choice is yours to make. What kind of woman do you want to be?

How important it is that we give refreshment to those around us and especially to those who are in His service! I hope we are never ashamed or embarrassed by someone's shortcoming or handicap. Instead we should seek to encourage all those God brings our way. Remember, we are providing essentials for others to grow. Do they leave your house refreshed? Record some ideas of how you can make your home encouraging.

Always Reflect:

The difference between reflect and remember is important to explain at this juncture. To remember is to bring something to mind again. I guess you could say it is bringing the past into the present, at least in your mind.

To reflect is "To have a bearing or influence; to make manifest or apparent." An example: "The pulse reflects the condition of the heart," according to Merriam-Webster.[1]

To be a person who always reflects is being a person who allows whatever is influencing you to bounce off of you and be reflected, like a mirror.

Thinking of water and air brings the concept of reflection. When you look in pond or a pool you see a reflection. The warm summer wind blowing through your hair can bring back memories of romantic times with someone special. Mirrors of course, also reflect. An important part of decorating is causing someone to reflect. Mirrors, fountains, and fire are three elements to definitely include in your design because all of these reflect or at least cause you to reflect.

II Corinthians 5:17 says, "Therefore, if anyone is in Christ, he is a new creation; the old has gone, the new has come!" We were made in the image of God, but if we are going to be someone who reflects the right things in our lives then we need to be becoming like Jesus. It is one thing to know Jesus as your Savior, it is completely another thing to become like Him. To become like Him starts with another "r" word – reconciliation. Colossians 1:21-22 says, "Once you were alienated from God and were enemies in your minds because of your evil behavior. But now he has reconciled you by Christ's physical body through death to present you holy in his sight, without blemish and free from accusation."

Notice that through reconciliation Christ is able to present you to God – perfect. And you didn't even have to try for perfection because Christ makes you complete. This is not to say that we make no effort. Our work is to focus on Him and He will create the new and improved us.

Colossians 3:2-10 says,

Set your minds on things above, not on earthly things. For you died, and your life is now hidden with Christ in God. When Christ, who is your life, appears, then you also will appear with him in glory. Put to death, therefore, whatever belongs to your earthly nature; sexual immorality, impurity, lust, evil desires and greed, which is idolatry. Because of these, the wrath of God is coming. You used to walk in these ways, in the life you once lived. But now you must rid yourselves of all such things as these; anger, rage, malice, slander, and filthy language from your lips. Do not lie to each other, since you have taken off your old self with its practices and have put on the new self, which is being renewed in knowledge in the image of its Creator.

So let me ask you a hard question. What is standing in your way? What have you not taken "off" that you need to get rid of in order to become that new creation?

Do you lie, even a little, or let filthy language come out of your mouth? Are you full of rage and show your anger? Do you slander or in malice try to hurt others? Maybe none of these show themselves on the outside but do any of them haunt your mind because you know you have thought them? What about lust? This is usually thought of as a man's sin, but in today's world where women have been in the workforce for a couple of decades the lust area has swayed to include us in its wake. Do you allow yourself to become emotionally attached to the opposite sex? Do you entertain "innocent" ideas of another man? How about just good old fashioned materialism? Do you live each day for what you can store away – keeping track of what your neighbor has that you want? Remember, the pulse reflects the condition of the heart. What exactly are you reflecting when people look at you? Take a few minutes and let God search your heart. Be honest with yourself and let Him change you with the ability to reflect His Son Jesus! There is freedom in obeying God! It is also good to know that our obedience is a sweet fragrance to God.

Spiritual Homework:

Honestly face where you are in the process of becoming who God wants you to be. Record some of the areas you feel you need to work on in your spiritual life:

CHAPTER SIX RECIPE: A CANDLE FIX

Need a Candle fix? Here is a way to make use of those old candles. Use candles that you are tempted to throw away or those that are almost finished burning. Using a knife and cutting board, cut the wax into medium pieces. Be careful as you are doing this - you could easily cut yourself. In order to make it a little safer, put the candle in the microwave for about 8 seconds. You can also heat the knife under hot water to help it slide through the wax more easily. Purchase wicks at Michaels or another craft store and attach the wick to the bottom of an old glass or old candle holder. Pile in the chunks of wax pieces you cut up earlier – keeping the wick coming up through the middle of the wax chunks. Cut the wick so that it is no more than one fourth of an inch above the wax. Light your candle! You can also take wax you have cut into pieces and put in drawers to make clothing smell fragrant. Use these same cut up pieces as potpourri for your entire house by putting them in a zip lock bag that has a few holes in it and placing these bags in your air vents around the house.

PART TWO

The Creatures of Design (Creation day 6)

Psalm 66:5, "Come and see what God has done, how awesome his works in man's behalf."

SOMETHING UNCOMMON

(Creation Day Six)

SUMMING UP ACCESSORIES

In the musical story of the Wizard of Oz, as the motley crew is being groomed for entry into the wizard's presence, Dorothy asks if they can dye her eyes to match her gown. What a brave request! However, bravery is the essence of the idea behind accessories. It is about personal taste and the satisfaction of putting on the finishing touches.

When you are ready to accessorize your room, you have reached the final step in the decorating process, and my favorite part. We have talked about the sensations of seeing, hearing, touching and smelling. We will talk about taste a little later. This chapter, however, has no actual "sensation" to refer to, but as everyone likes to refer to the "sixth" sense – accessories could fall into this category. Everyone has some ability to decorate and this is where you really get to let your personality shine! This is no time to hold back – let go and have a great time being truly creative. We have a few details to work out before we get to incorporate accessories into our project so let's take care of these now.

Designer's Workshop:

"And God said, 'Let the land produce living creatures according to their kinds; livestock, creatures that move along the ground, and wild animals, each according to its kind.' And it was so" (Gen. 1:24).

God started out on the sixth day of creation by creating animals, in this order:

1. Livestock
2. Creatures that move along the ground
3. Wild animals

This is an excellent order to follow for decorating your room. Think of livestock as the larger pieces of furniture: couches, armoires, and beds. Next we come to creatures that move along the ground. These are rugs and small furniture like end tables and coffee tables. These will have to be placed in the room before we can bring in the wild animals –or in other words, our accessories!

Before you move in any of your livestock or ground creatures, make sure they are how you want them to be. Do they need to be painted, or covered? Fix them before you bring them into the room.

Furniture Placement

As you begin planning the arrangement of your furniture, let your mind become totally objective. Change your perspective by standing in the corner of the room, or better yet, pretend you are in someone else's house. Then you will have a better perspective of what the room really looks like. Decide the main function of the room. Is it a family room, a kitchen to eat in, or a formal living room to hold conversation with others? Write down the main function of the room on a piece of paper and tape it to a wall or door where it will be easy to see. It is amazing how often it is necessary to remind yourself how the room will be used in order to get the furniture placement correct. Writing it down helps!

As you put the furniture back into the room, make sure the main function of the room can occur. Wherever possible, keep the furniture away from the walls! Do cows all stand around the perimeter of the field? No, of course not! They group together in nice little conversational groups. Using

> Ancient Egypt: Often, chair leg design was influenced by animals. The chair's front legs were designed to look like an animal's front legs, while the chair's back legs looked like the animal's hind legs.

graph paper, draw the floor area of your room. Then, using a different piece of graph paper, make squares and rectangles to represent your furniture. You can rearrange to your heart's content to see all the different ways your room could work.

Personalize your Space

Now we can talk about the "Wild Animals." Divide accessories into four main groups to make it easier for identification.

1. Pictures, paintings, and photographs
2. Statues, and larger freestanding items
3. Smaller knick-knack items

4. Pillows and other fabric items

The biggest mistake most people make when choosing accessories is gathering items that are too small. Even in a smaller house it will look more complete and less cluttered if you choose one large accessory for an area rather than several small ones. The same can be said for pictures, the bigger the better. I have yet to see a really large picture and say, "That doesn't look right for the space because it's too big."

> Designer Thinking: Choose large items to accessorize.

Accessorizing is using the ability to color outside the lines. It is our tendency to pick the same types of things we always have chosen. Challenge yourself to venture outside your normal selections while you accessorize your room. Start the process by cutting out magazine pictures of rooms you like. You do not need to like every single aspect of the room in the magazine in order to choose it. The room in the picture may have only one item you like in it. Cut it out anyway and attach all the pictures you have chosen to your planning page. Decide what elements in the room make you like that particular room: is it the type of fabric in the windows, is it the stuff they put on the coffee table, or the kind of pillows on the couch? Write down some of the things you are drawn to in the magazine pictures.

The goal is to create a similar look in your room, using the pictures as a guide. But remember, you are not shopping to find the exact same object for your room. You are merely looking for something comparable.

I would suggest you begin accessorizing by looking at second-hand stores for unique items. Fill in the rest of your spaces by looking in regular stores. Don't forget to go "shopping" in

---

Jana's Tip for Hanging Pictures—The SPH Way

1. Hold the picture where you think it should be mounted.
2. Use one hand to hold the picture while you use the other hand to find the mount point (usually a mounting wire or bracket) behind the picture.
3. Press the mount point down on your finger so that when the picture is removed, you can see an indentation of the mount point on your finger. Using this indentation as a reference, use a pencil with your other hand to mark the location for the nail or anchor.
4. Install the first nail or anchor in the place you have marked with a pencil.
5. If your picture requires two nails or anchors, hang the picture on the nail or anchor you have already installed, and complete steps 7 and 8 below.
6. Put a level on the top of the picture frame and adjust to level.
7. Feel behind the side that still needs a nail. Repeat step 4-6.

---

the rest of the rooms in your house. You may find something you are tired of in one room that will really add the finishing touches to the room you are working on. Quite often decorating becomes expensive because someone is being too picky. The pickier you are, the more money you are going to spend. Most of the time there is an item that will accomplish the same effect that costs less than the original idea or inspiration. This is how I save the majority of money in my decorating projects. Look at your magazine pictures and the items that appeal to you. What is it about them that really grabs your attention – does the item look old, is it the size or shape of the object, is it the placement of a number of items? Make a plan to create the effect you desire in a less expensive way. And make sure to have fun!

Sometimes we tend to get "stuck" in a decade. It usually shows up the most in our accessories. For those of you who may be stuck in the "eighties," you have two choices:

1. You should be made aware that it is now in style to be stuck in the sixties and seventies.
2. But if you would rather – hang in there I'm sure we'll make it back around to the 80's if you wait. (Hair styles and clothes are already back!) Because what goes around – goes around and around and around!

Matthew 6:19-21 says, "Do not store up for yourselves treasures on earth, where moth and rust destroy, and where thieves break in and steal. But store up for yourselves treasures in heaven, where moth and rust do not destroy, and where thieves do not break in and steal. For where your treasure is, there your heart will be also."

Sometimes the reason people get stuck in a "time warp" is because they are clinging too much to their earthly possessions. I'm not saying you have to get rid of Great-Grandma's silver, or Aunt Ida's jewelry collection she passed down to you at graduation. Balance is the key in all areas of life. It doesn't hurt, however, to assess the things you are holding on to as we keep heaven in mind. Are they really necessary? Do they really mean that much to you, or do you have plenty of mementos with which to remember Granny? Remain flexible with your possessions to maximize your creative ability.

How to be creative with accessories

Be creative with:

1. Raw Materials
2. Placement of objects
3. Usage
4. Color
5. Size

I have the most fun accessorizing with items I use in an unconventional fashion. Entire books have been written with ideas of how to reuse and fix up. Pick up a couple of decorating books or magazines and see what ideas you

> If God can make people out of dust, I can make a pan-rack out of a futon frame!

can borrow. Using outdoor objects (like garden gates) for inside decorating is often very fun and inexpensive. Don't forget – large items pack more of a punch.

Remember, "Earth Protocol" can get in the way of being creative. Thoughts like, don't eat cake for breakfast and don't leave the price tag on a gift can really restrict the mind from bending in other areas. (Just a side note, how come it is thought of as rude to leave a price tag on a gift that may say $5, but it is ok to give a $5 bill in a card as a gift? And how come one shies away from eating cake for breakfast, but will eat a cake donut? Just a thought!)

It is now time to take a second look at the three groups you organized in the first chapter:

1. Garage Sale
2. Useable items
3. Items with potential

Perhaps you already got rid of the garage sale items. Good for you! Take a look again at your useable items. These are items that belong in the room the same way a coffee maker belongs in the kitchen, or a TV belongs in the family room. Make sure you have what you need for your room. The last section is the fun section – items with potential. These are accessories you may have had for a long time. You enjoy them, but they may need a face lift. We have talked about some of them in the first lesson, but now we really need to get serious about them. Do they need to be painted? Do they need new fabric, or both? Now is the time to get busy.

Design Homework:

- Cut out pictures in magazines of rooms that have the feel you desire to accomplish in your room.
- Reassess the items in the "Items with potential" section from the first lesson.
- Try shopping at some secondhand or thrift stores for other unique items.
- Finish up by shopping at regular stores for necessary new items (like towels).

Spiritual Thinking:

As we discussed earlier, some of us are cherishing accessories God cannot use:

Lack of forgiveness
Pride
Selfish ambition
Hatred
Sexual impurity
Discord

Jealousy
Envy

We need to take these useless accessories and put them in the "Throw-away" pile of our spiritual lives. The Bible teaches us about "Spiritual Armor." After Adam and Eve sinned in the Garden of Eden, God clothed them to cover what was revealed to them as nakedness. As we come to this part of our spiritual journey, we need to have a specific kind of clothing to keep these useless accessories from resurfacing in our lives. This spiritual armor should be at the top of your list for spiritual accessories.

Ephesians 6:10-17 says:

> Finally, be strong in the Lord and in the strength of His might. Put on the full armor of God, so that you will be able to stand firm against the schemes of the devil. For our struggle is not against flesh and blood, but against the rulers, against the powers, against the world forces of this darkness, against the spiritual forces of wickedness in the heavenly places. Therefore, take up the full armor of God, so that you will be able to resist in the evil day, and having done everything, to stand firm. Stand firm therefore, having girded your loins with truth, and having put on the breastplate of righteousness, and having shod your feet with the preparation of the Gospel of Peace; in addition to all, taking up the Shield of Faith with which you will be able to extinguish all the flaming arrows of the evil one. And take the Helmet of Salvation and the Sword of the Spirit, which is the Word of God.

God gave us unique personalities that He wants us to use, but He also wants us to develop our spiritual strengths so that we will be able to defeat evil. If we don't develop our spiritual strengths, we will be ineffective in our spiritual lives. What are you allowing God to create in you? Without implementing the armor of God our lives are like a room without accessories. We are left with a very boring outcome that does not reach its full potential. Take the time to pray "on" each piece of equipment. When we "put on" the full armor of God, we are "putting on" Jesus, and Jesus really knows how to accessorize life!

Spiritual Homework:

- Pray the armor of God on every day this next week.

Belt of Truth: We get truth from God's Word. The more we know what the Bible has to say about God then we will be confident knowing who He is and what He expects from us. We can pray, *God, help me to understand what I read in your Word today so that I can apply it to my life and live the way You want me to live. Help me learn more about You today.*

Breastplate of Righteousness: We have no righteousness of our own, but if we know Jesus as our Savior, He covers us with His righteousness and that is what God sees when He looks at us. You may have times when you feel that you have gone too far for the grace of God to reach, and the enemy will try to tell you that you are not righteous in God's eyes. But if you have asked Jesus to be your Savior, no one can take that righteousness away. There are times when we need to make things right with God, but His righteousness never leaves us even when we are in need of some spiritual correction in our lives. *God, thank you that my righteousness is dependant on your truth rather than my actions. Help me remember this so that I can live the way You want me to live.*

Feet Covered with the Gospel of Peace: When we live in light of the gift of salvation, it makes us live at peace with one another. As we walk through life with this at the forefront of our minds, it makes it rather difficult to get mad at the long lines in grocery stores or the waitress messing up our order. With the big picture in mind everything else is trivial.

We can pray, *God, help me to live in peace with others today. Help me to point them in the direction of Your salvation. Help me be a good example. Lead me down the right paths today and help me keep Your salvation in mind as I come into contact with others.*

The Shield of Faith: This shield has one main purpose – to fight off the lies of Satan. The enemy will try to make you doubt and doubt is the opposite of faith. The Shield of Faith should be correctly placed to fight against these "fiery darts" intended to sidetrack. The enemy wants you to think you are insignificant and incapable as a Christian. The fact is, you can't do it by yourself – that is why you are relying on God – or having Faith in His plan – Jesus. So keep the Shield of Faith in place to fight against the urge to believe the lies that you will hear:

- You don't measure up
- You don't deserve God
- He doesn't need you or want you
- He is tired of your complaining.

Let's Pray: *God, thank You for Your gift of Salvation. Help me to keep the Shield of Faith in place because of Christ's sacrifice on the cross. Because of Jesus I pray against Satan and his lies – let them bounce off my shield of faith as I remember all day what You have given me and I cast doubt aside. Thank You – in Jesus' name AMEN.*

The Helmet of Salvation: A helmet is for one main purpose – to protect the head and in this case, the mind. We need to protect what we allow to come into our minds. Most sin happen in the mind, where only you and God are witnesses. Some of those habits are hard to break because they are easily hidden from your peers. Once again, keeping salvation at the forefront of our thoughts will help us kick out any sinful thoughts that try to creep in. These could include jealousy, lust, lack of forgiveness, and pride. It is easy to think that our personal thoughts can't hurt anyone, but they do hurt someone. They hurt God's feelings because He sent His Son so that we could stop being so filled up with wrong thoughts. These secret sins also hurt us. It is unhealthy for us to hold on to these thoughts. We need to remove these hurtful things and replace them with God's best plan for our spiritual journey. If you had cancerous tumor, and the doctors were able to remove it, you would have them operate. Likewise, you will want to remove these sins "of the mind" because God says they are bad for you.

Let's Pray: *God, bring to my mind things I dwell on that are not what You want me to think about. I confess them to you as sin and ask that if they return, You will remind me that they are not pleasing thoughts to You. I can choose to think about better things that will benefit my relationship with You. Thank you God for protecting my mind with the Helmet of Salvation.*

The Sword of the Spirit: This sword is the Word of God. Swords are for fighting and our spiritual sword is meant for spiritual battle. We need to continually stay in the Word of God as this is our only offensive spiritual weapon.

We can pray, *God, thank You for Your Word – please bring to mind today the scriptures that I need to stay focused on what You have for me today. Your words are more powerful than my own.*

This is a powerful way to start each day. It is the best recipe for living!

CHAPTER SEVEN RECIPE: HOW TO MAKE A "SAVE PERFECTION FOR HEAVEN" COAT RACK

I love unusual accessories, but I also love it when accessories are not only unusual, but useful. One of the most useful items you can put in your house is a coat rack. You can make a coat rack out of almost any kind of material. You need a flat piece of wood—it could be a piece of molding or an old boat oar. This will be the back of the coat hanger. Then purchase hooks—many places have coat hooks. You can find coat hooks at Target or sometimes in the toy-box. You can use small toys for hooks by drilling holes and attaching them to the mounting board. Or you can buy more efficient hooks for hanging clothing items by getting actual hooks and mounting those to the flat piece of wood. Once you have your coat hooks assembled they can be used for many reasons. You can use them in your children's rooms for hanging bags of toys or dress-up clothes. They can be placed in laundry rooms to hang clothes hanger bags or jackets or any number of items. The possibilities are limitless as to what you could use them for—but one thing is for sure—if you make it unusual, it is more fun to use for everyday items.

Psalm 40:4a says "Blessed is the man who makes the Lord his trust."

THE MAN YOU FACTOR . . .

(. . . into your decorating project)

Men, can't decorate with them, can't decorate without their money! So what to do about the man you factor into your decorating project?

There's a man in my house

You will never hear a little girl playing house say to her brother, "Now, come back here and put your trucks by the front door where they belong!" She's usually yelling at him, "Get out of here you'll mess everything up!" In our ideal playhouse we never made an allotment for the male presence. It wasn't part of the equation.

In our early years of play-acting, we were the ones in charge. Now our plans are really messed up. Too often our minds, if not our mouths, are shouting, "Get out of here, you're messing everything up!" So the first acknowledgment we have to make is "There's a man in my house." We've got to get used to the idea, so if you have not embraced this you better say it out loud right now—"There's a man in my house." It's a simple realization, but acknowledging it helps the mind accept that things may not be the way we have planned.

Realization #1: *There's a man in my house!*

THERE'S A CAKE IN THE GARAGE

Watching a small boy play with cars is very entertaining. He makes no room for cakes or dishes in his play garage and certainly doesn't have to wait for a lady passenger to put her seatbelt on before zooming out of the driveway and down the street. I can't count the number of times I had to remind my husband to go easy on the speed bumps when I was pregnant. It's a wonder all of the kids weren't born three months early. It put somewhat of a cramp in his style, because he had to slow down – literally.

Boys are independent, happy go lucky, ready to play at the drop of a hat. Anything can be a gun, and they can start play in less than three seconds flat. A little girl, on the other hand, has to do some planning. She sets up all her dolls and dishes and then it is time to start playing. That is, unless her brother has just bulldozed his way through her garden party because one minute ago he decided it was time to play. He may or may not have anticipated her response. You can tell which, by the smile of satisfaction or by the look of complete bewilderment. Whatever the case, you may be assured of one thing. When your man was a little boy playing with his cars, he did not stop to open the door for a pretend wife. He did not slow down for speed bumps or turn the corner slowly out of consideration for his future passengers. He just played, like we girls did when we played house. Although we planned on being married someday, we didn't plan for them; and although they planned on driving a real car someday, they didn't plan on taking us along with them. We need to realize we messed up their plans too!

I think men and boys understand how to play better than females. I watch my husband play with the children. He really gets in there and plays. Sometimes I will say, "Now be careful of..." Really, I mean everything, even if I only mention one item. He usually says, "Oh, we're just having fun don't spoil it."

I can't take myself out of the "mother/ grown up" role when I play. I am constantly doing the things mothers do: preventing glasses of milk from spilling, vases from breaking, the bird from being eaten by the dog, the baby from being landed on, and last but not least, my husband from playing too hard and hurting one of the kids.

Whether you like it or not, the roles are divided from birth. Men and women are different. These differences bring humor and interest to life, or at least they should. But when those differences show up in the area of decorating it is challenging. Maybe they see no need to spend the money on decorating or maybe he can't seem to agree on any of the choices you give him. Perhaps he's being unkind by saying he doesn't like any of your choices or your style. His mother had the house the same way for thirty years and it was just fine. Or he fancies himself an expert on style and says he likes his own style better than yours.

Realization #2: *They have different plans than we do.*

In our human nature, we did not see beyond ourselves as children. As adults some of our attitudes need to change. Let me ask you, are your decorating desires draining the life out of your family? You cannot change your spouse, as you probably already know. The more you allow God to conform you to the image of His Son, the less conflict you will experience with your spouse – even if he doesn't get the decorating thing at all. God has given men the awesome responsibility of being the head of the house. I Corinthians 11:3 says, "Now I want you to realize that the head of every man is Christ, and the head of the woman is man, and the head of Christ is God." It becomes evident we do not think like God, because not only did He make a place for men in daily living, He put them in charge!

Realization #3: *God put them in charge.*

So, what can we do? Pray for your man! Pray for him to be a man after God's own heart. Pray for him to be pure. Pray for him to love God with all of his heart and with all of his soul and with his entire mind. And pray that God will help him to have an understanding mind when it comes to the decorating of your home.

There are basically three kinds of husbands when it comes to decorating:

1. The husband that tells you to do whatever you want.
2. The husband that tells you to do whatever you want, then complains about everything you do.
3. The husband who wants to be totally included in all of the decorating process.

What do we do with these men in our lives who insist on being a part of it? How does God want us to respond when the man of the house wants to be the man of interior design? What about the man who just grunts and says with indifference, "Whatever you want, dear." Are there any ideal men out there when it comes to decorating? You know the kind - He smiles with approval at every paint chip and fabric swatch you bring home, and hangs on your every word as you describe in detail all the different choices and what kind of look you are trying to create in **your** space. He lovingly hands over the checkbook and walks you to the door. With a smile and a warm embrace he tells you to have a wonderful time shopping, spend as much as you want, and take as long as you need because he is watching the kids.

Well, as many of us have discovered, these men exist only in fairytales, movies made for women, and our own preconceived notions. Let's face it; the man God made is far different from the one we would have created. It's a good thing God made the woman after He made man or the woman would have been telling God how to create her husband. When learning how to relate to our man in the area of decorating, we need to remember how God made the man. What is the man's main job and what are his gifts? How does he process through a project – or does he process at all?

You're Married – Get over it!

Jack and Jill went up the hill to fetch a pail of water. Jack fell down and broke his crown and Jill went the other way hoping nobody saw her with the guy who fell down. Although it sounds like a cliché, I would have to say that marriage is a mindset. There are two mindsets to choose from. The first one we will look at is the human mindset.

The Human Mindset says:

- I deserve the best, so I will keep trying until I find someone who meets all my needs.
- If he looks good and can provide for me in the manner to which I am accustomed, then I might spend the rest of my life with him – if I don't get tired of him.
- If he embarrasses me one more time – that's it!

143

- I loved him when we were first married, but I have fallen out of love with him.
- I thought I loved him but I am just now learning what real love is – and I don't love him – so that's that.
- I want to grow and improve myself and he just wants to stay the same. We just don't have anything in common any more, so it's over.

These sound reasonable to our human thinking. You will notice in reading the statements above, the perspective is from an outsider looking in. The woman is solo, reviewing the situation. She is judge, jury, and executioner. She is not deciding something with her husband, but deciding something for them by herself. She is not a "them," but a "her." Once you are married, you are to be a "them." She has separated herself mentally from her marriage.

Let's take the children's poem about Jack and Jill for instance. They are probably supposed to be brother and sister, but let's pretend they are a married couple. What do you think happened after the embarrassing falling down episode? I can just see Jill over at Susan's house.

"And do you know what happened next? He fell right down – he didn't even see that rock – it was right in front of him."

Susan replies, "Jack's a nice guy, but when is he going to grow up! I mean, you have been married for two years and these falling down things have been going on long enough. I don't know how you put up with it."

"I know," says Jill, "I'm just not sure it's working out. I used to go tumbling after, but I've grown and he still seems to be the same old Jack. Maybe it's time for me to move on."

Things happen in marriage that make us feel the same as Jill. The combining of hearts in a ceremony of marriage does not include the combining of minds. What one person considers perfectly fine, his or her spouse may view as completely absurd. Several years ago my husband traveled a lot for his job and was gone for three or four days at a time. He had been gone for several days working, just like he always did, and he came home, just like he always did. I went to meet him at the door and welcomed him home, but what met me did not resemble the man I married! My husband was thirty-five, straight teeth, beautiful black hair, and brown eyes. Very handsome! The man who met me was bald! Completely bald! I stopped short—I didn't even hug him. I couldn't bring myself to look at him for days. Everything in me mentally disassociated from him. It wasn't a conscience act – it just happened. I was so mad at him for shaving his head, and I wasn't very happy with God either. I said to God, "How could you let me marry this man?"

We all have times like this in marriage don't we? When you are in an argument with someone, you are not together with them. Instead, you are opponents trying to win a war. You have separated yourself from him. "Just who does he think he is?" "See if I ever do anything for him again – I was just trying to be helpful," or "He wasn't thinking about anyone but himself." These are the thoughts that come to mind, mirroring the Human Mindset.

When this happens, we disconnect from our husbands. Something has bothered or even embarrassed us to the point that we don't want to even be identified with them. Everyone does this at times, but what concerns me is the number of women who stay in a disconnected state of mind. God sees them as **one** and they are **one** physically. The laws of this country view them as **one** unit, but they have not fully relinquished individual rights to identify themselves with another.

As a Christian, my overall identity is in Jesus Christ. 2 Corinthians 5:17 says, "Therefore, if anyone is in Christ, he is a new creation; the old has gone, the new has come!" My earthly identification, if I am married, is with my spouse. Marriage is to be a picture of the relationship with God. Christ is not ashamed to completely identify Himself with us, even though we are not perfect. He even died for us so He could identify with us.

While Christ lived on the earth, He showed many different kinds of human emotion. He had compassion (Luke 7:13). He cried (John 11:35). He was overwhelmed (Matt. 26:37,38). He grieved (Mark 3:5). But I find no mention of him being embarrassed by his disciples, mother, or brothers. Even when Peter disassociated himself from Jesus and denied knowing him, Jesus was still willing to be identified with Peter. Jesus shows no signs of being embarrassed, although he displayed a myriad of other emotions. I have to ask – Why not embarrassment? Is embarrassment an emotion or is it simply a nice word for sin? Jesus was human, and had human emotion just like us – yet he was without sin. (Heb. 4:15). I find that the hidden element behind my embarrassment most of the time is **pride**. What will they think? How do I look? I can't believe I said that – it must have sounded dumb. So what is it that makes us want to separate ourselves from our husbands?

Disassociation is a slow and silent killer of a good relationship. The worst part about it is that we allow it, and even invite it into our hearts and minds by what we watch on TV or read in paperback romance books. A woman will mentally "free" herself from her man so that when he does the things that embarrass her, she no longer feels that it reflects badly on her. In her mind, however, this leaves her in a precarious place. It makes her think of herself as *available*. One does not wake up one morning and decide to have an affair. It begins with lies that are considered, then embraced, then acted upon. But before the lies can ever have an effect – first comes discontentment and disassociation from the spouse. This is a trap Satan uses against unsuspecting housewives. This trap has many different faces, and pride is the element Satan uses to implement his device of disassociation. I believe the first degree of disassociation could be called a knee-jerk reaction. Like my reaction to my husband's bald head. That same night he came home with the bald head, we went to Wal-Mart as a family because we needed some things. I didn't even want him to go to the store with us, but he had the money, so I let him come along. We had just gotten out of the car and were walking through the parking lot when I noticed another young couple coming towards us. It was dark and I was so embarrassed by the way my husband looked that I didn't really look at them. I said to God, "Help him notice how this couple thinks he looks weird." I watched the woman as we passed by ready for the strange look she was sure to give my bald husband. She looked at him, but made no expression at all. I looked up at the couple confused. Then I saw her husband – young, good-looking, and you guessed it – bald. "Very funny," I said to God.

I got the point though. My reaction of shock was warranted because James came home with a bald head! I wasn't used to it and he didn't warn me about it on the phone – it was a shock. But now it was up to me. I could hang on to my disconnected state, or I could choose a willful act of re-associating with my husband – bald head and all. My irritated mind was saying, "When all your hair grows back, then I will act, talk and feel like your wife, but until then, I am on vacation!" That thinking is conditional however, and my vows said "for better or worse." Of course, I envisioned growing old together and if that meant gray hair or no hair – fine. But this was on purpose and he didn't seem to care how it made me feel! He didn't do it to spite me however, and it was not done maliciously or with ill intent, so the problem belonged to me. I needed to implement something I had learned a very long time ago, not from my marriage, but from my parents' divorce. For me, it is always the first step back toward re-associating with my husband. We will conclude with that after we take a little detour.

Save Perfection For Heaven

CAN A DEAD MARRIAGE BE GOOD?

I love to go to garage sales. I love to see what treasure I can find. One day I was "treasure hunting" and came upon a wedding dress hanging on the door to the garage. A note was pinned to the dress, so I drew near to see what was written on the paper. It said "Worn only once, by mistake."

If everyone were honest, they would have to admit that at least one time in their marriage, they felt they had made a mistake by marrying their mate. Even the most loving couples have times of doubt and insecurity in their union – after all, we would feel better if our spouses liked everything about us and never had a complaint. It would be nice if we always agreed on everything, specifically design. But I can only think of one married couple who has never had a disagreement:

A MAN MARRIED A CORPSE AND SPENT A "HONEYMOON" NIGHT WITH HER!

Antonio Puno, a security guard at the presidential palace, married Editha Reyes, as she lay in a coffin in the church. It was a funeral-wedding ceremony the local people will never forget.

The coffin bearing Edith in her wedding gown entered the church as scheduled. Her father was beside the coffin. Ahead was Edith's godson who acted as ring-bearer. The rest of the bridal entourage followed. Waiting at the altar was Tony, who stood at the head of Edith's coffin as the Protestant pastor officiated.

When it was all over, the glass top of the coffin was lifted. He kissed her on the forehead and the cheek, while those near the coffin flinched at the strong smell of chemicals. The wedding ended. The dirge was played. The funeral began. Tony spent the night at Edith's house, describing it as "my honeymoon night." He said he placed Edith's tangerine duster close to his chest as he lay remembering their days together.

Tony and Edith went steady in 1970. It was a long engagement. Four days before Edith's death, they finally set the wedding date for June 28th. And then tragedy struck. Edith had a slight fever and hard time breathing. The town doctor was called who immediately gave her a shot of dimpheril. Within five minutes she became pale and was brought to the hospital. The next day, Edith was dead.

Before she succumbed, she was able to whisper to Tony: "If I die, will the wedding still be held?" Tony confided he said "Yes." [2]

I can guarantee you that Edith had no problem agreeing with her husband. She never opened her mouth when she wasn't supposed to, and those irritating things all husbands do did not bother her one bit. Something her husband did or said never embarrassed her and she never had to re-associate herself to him. Of course, the reason why she didn't struggle with any of these things was because she was dead!

But that is what we are supposed to be – dead to sin, and alive to God. Romans 6:11 says "In the same way, count yourselves dead to sin but alive to God in Christ Jesus." My mom used to say, "Well, I want to be dead to sin, but I just keep sitting up in my casket."

We spoke earlier of things that lead to our wanting to disassociate from our husbands. In the case of embarrassment, is it a sin or just an emotion? Well, one thing is for sure. It is not one of the fruits of the Spirit (Gal. 5:20,21). I believe embarrassment is a temptation, but to be tempted is not sin. Temptation is just the idea to do something wrong, and at that point you can choose to sin or you can resist temptation. Jesus was tempted (Luke 4:1-13), but he turned away from temptation and did not sin. The other temptations that cause us to pull away from our union are: anger (I hate it when he leaves the toilet seat up), disapproval (I knew it was a mistake to buy that new car), fear (what if we can't make the house payment), self- sufficiency (I don't want you to help me decorate, I can do it myself), self-indulgence (I don't want to make your lunch – I'm watching my TV show), self-pity (I can't believe he won't let me paint the room the color I want), and last of all – pride (I deserved a better husband than him).

Pride is the king of all sins. The very first sin ever committed was pride. Here is the account of that sin which was committed by Satan: Isaiah 14:12-14 says, "How you have fallen from heaven, O morning star, son of the dawn! You have been cast down to the earth, you who once laid low the nations! You said in your heart, 'I will ascend to heaven; I will raise my throne above the stars of God; I will sit enthroned on the mount of assembly, on the utmost heights of the sacred mountain. I will ascend above the tops of the clouds; I will make myself like the Most High.'"

I have yet to find a sin you cannot trace back to pride. The sin of pride takes place in the mind, which is why I said the battle is a mindset. When the temptation comes – "I don't want to see my husband until his hair grows back"—we can yield to the temptation by doing what it suggests, or we can "die" to our natural feelings (pride) and, following Christ's example, by being willing to associate with our spouse. Now that can be hard. Would you like to know a secret that makes it easier?

I mentioned earlier that I learned an important lesson from my parents' divorce. I was thirteen when I received my first lesson. My mom and I had been in an argument and there was not another adult there to counterbalance her decision. I will never forget this day as long as I live. We were standing in my doorway – eyeball to eyeball – in the heat of disagreement. It was like time stopped for a short moment and I realized I would not make it for another five or six years under her roof if I did not have help. It was not that mom was a bad mom or that I was an awful child, but we were both human. I prayed silently to God. *Please help me – give me Your kind of love for her or I will not make it!* Immediately, I felt an overwhelming love for her like none I had ever known. There was no doubt that God had answered my prayer, and mom and I are still great friends.

God's Mindset says:

- God puts up with me when I don't deserve it. I need to be patient and loving toward my spouse even when he doesn't deserve it.
- Life is not perfect – we fight sometimes. Sometimes we get tired of each other, but I made a promise and God wants to help me keep that promise. So I will choose to love the person I married.
- He does some pretty silly things – still acts like a boy sometimes. I will choose to identify myself with him the way Christ is willing to be in my life even though I still make mistakes.
- I don't always feel "love" feelings for my husband the way I used to, but I know that my human love will fail and real love comes from God. I will ask God to help me love my husband.
- I Corinthians 13:4-8a, "Love is patient, love is kind. It does not envy, it does not boast, it is not proud. It is not rude, it is not self-seeking, it is not easily angered, it keeps no record of wrongs. Love does not delight in evil but rejoices with the truth. It always protects, always trusts, always hopes, always perseveres. Love never fails."

So here was what I learned: Love is not natural. Real love and real romance come from knowing and loving God personally. He will then bring into your life the things that will glorify Him. When someone has completely surrendered at the feet of Jesus and they desire something that is in His will, He always gives it to them. Did God want me to love my mother? Of course! I wanted to be in His will and He gave me what I asked for immediately and without reserve. So the love one human can have for another in this life can be the eternal love that was shown to us on the cross. It is there if we ask.

Most people believe love for their relatives comes naturally, but God's Word says that naturally we are wicked (Jer. 17:9). Naturally we are selfish. In contrast I Corinthians 13 says, "Love is patient, love is kind. It does not envy, it does not boast, it is not proud. It is not rude, it is not self-seeking, it is not easily angered, it keeps no record of wrongs . . . It never fails."

The love I brought into my marriage failed because it is not God's love, it was just human love – you know – I love ice cream! I began to realize that just as I couldn't make it for five or six more years with mom – I certainly couldn't make it until death do us part with my own kind of love. I just didn't have the ability to love my husband without God giving me His love for James and without His grace to do my part in the Holy union He ordained.

We are naturally selfish in our love, and we often love others because it makes us feel better about ourselves. It feels good to have a boyfriend because it makes us feel like we are part of the liveliness of the world. It is nice to have someone paying attention to us. But when God gives us His love, it is pure, it is selfless, and it is a love that completes rather than depletes.

We have the right to ask the Father for anything in the name of Jesus Christ, our Savior. So I asked for love, and He gave it to me. Being able to love someone even when they disappoint you – that is God's love. Asking for love is the right start in the direction of God's mindset for marriage.

God promises a lot of things. He promises He will not give you any trials that are too hard for you to handle (I Cor. 10:13). He promises to be your strength, and that He will never leave you (Heb. 13:5b). He does not, however, promise that the man you marry will always be someone you can look up to, admire, and respect. He tells us to respect our husbands, but He did not promise that the person we marry would be deserving of respect. God also promised we would have trials in our lives. Sometimes husbands fall into the category of trials! He wants us to become more like Jesus, and He will use those trials to help us become more like Him (Rom. 8:28,29). And decorating with husbands usually falls into the category of trials. Here are three things that can help in this process of decorating with the man you choose to love.

THREE PRINCIPLES TO USE WHEN DECORATING WITH MY HUSBAND

1. I have to willingly re-associate with my husband every time I am tempted to disassociate.
2. I need to admit that if my husband really doesn't like something – I wouldn't want it in my home anyway. (So let go of it).
3. Sure-fire way to get what you want and keep your man happy:

   - Let him make the final decision.
     "Honey, I bought these three lamps. I like them all and I thought you could make the final decision and I will return the other two."
   - Embrace the decision he makes.
     "Oh, I am so glad you picked that one – it is the best lamp!"
   - Choose to make his decision your own.
     It is easier to do this when you only give them choices you really can live with. Then they are making a decision you like. If you realize that you don't like one of the choices you gave him – and that is the

one he chooses – grin and bear it! Then decide to like it.

CHAPTER EIGHT RECIPE: HOW TO KEEP YOUR MAN HAPPY: MAKE COOKIES!

¾ cup brown sugar
¾ cup white sugar
1 cup margarine

Cream together then add:

One egg
1-2 Tbsp vanilla

Stir these together then add the following dry ingredients:

2 ¼ cups flour
1 tsp baking soda
Add chocolate chips or white chocolate chips or butterscotch chips. Or any kind of candy you want.
Bake at 350 degrees for 9-12 minutes.

Psalm 65:4b says, "We are filled with the good things of your house."

SAVOR THE FLAVOR

(Creation Day Six Contd.)

Ahh food! Need I really say more? We can't seem to get enough of two things in this life, good food and good conversation. Food really does speak for itself. If you have people over and set food in front of them – they know it is for them to enjoy. Even if you don't set it out for them, some guests will go in search of food if they feel comfortable enough in your home. As I have said, that is a sign that you are a good hostess!

Let's look at how God finished the creation of the world. Genesis 1:26-31 says

> Then God said, "Let us make man in our image, in our likeness, and let them rule over the fish of the sea and the birds of the air, over the livestock, over all the earth, and over all the creatures that move along the ground." So God created man in his own image, in the image of God he created him; male and female he created them. God blessed them and said to them, "Be fruitful and increase in number; fill the earth and

subdue it. Rule over the fish of the sea and the birds of the air and over every living creature that moves on the ground." Then God said, "I give you every seed-bearing plant on the face of the whole earth and every tree that has fruit with seed in it. They will be yours for food. And to all the beasts of the earth and all the birds of the air and all the creatures that move on the ground – everything that has the breath of life in it. I give every green plant for food." And it was so. God saw all that he had made, and it was very good. And there was evening, and there was morning – the sixth day.

The very last thing God created was mankind, and the very first thing He provided for them was food to eat. Remember this was before mankind had chosen to sin, so the animals were friendly with the people and everyone seemed to be vegetarian. Let's look at a couple of other passages in the Bible that refer to hospitality:

- Romans 12:13, "Share with God's people who are in need. Practice hospitality." Are we only to share with people in need? Romans goes on to say in verse 14, "Bless those who persecute you; bless and do not curse." When was the last time you were hospitable to someone who mistreated you?
- I Peter 4:9, "Offer hospitality to one another without grumbling."
- Galatians 6:10, "Therefore, as we have opportunity, let us do good to all people, especially to those who belong to the family of believers."

The Bible does not say to offer hospitality only:

- If you feel like it
- To people you really like
- If you have the gift of hospitality

God gives everyone the command to be hospitable. For some of you, this is easy. For others it is stretching out of your comfort zone. It's ok if you have not fully developed this area of your life, but challenge yourself to be who God wants you to be.

There is another side of me that struggles with hospitality at times. And believe it or not, it has to do with my own family! It is easier for me to be hospitable to others than my own household. Sad, but true! Well, this is how it happens. I spend all day cleaning, or get a special decorating project completed – completed mind you – that means it's done. Unless someone undoes it! Which, they often do – of course I am referring to the shorter people who abide in my house. Quite often after I am finished with something, in come the younger members of the family to prove I was wrong. I hate redoing something! Once I have completed a project I love to stand back and admire my work, and then in they come and ruin it! How dare they! And it's not just the children, sometimes it's the other half, or visitors. Sometimes it's the ones you are trying to be hospitable to – and you say through clenched teeth and fake smile, "That's ok, I was going to use the steam cleaner anyway." It's hard to be hospitable! Life looks beautiful, and then you add people and they mess it up! But I guarantee you – God understands!

Let's look at Genesis 3

> Then the man and his wife heard the sound of the Lord God as he was walking in the garden in the cool of the day, and they hid from the Lord God among the trees of the garden. But the Lord God called to the man, "Where are you?" He answered, "I heard you in the garden, and I was afraid because I was naked; so I hid." And he said, "Who told you that you were naked? Have you eaten from the tree that I commanded you not to eat from?" Genesis 3:8-11.

God made a beautiful garden home for two perfect people and they messed it up! Believe me, if two perfect people still managed to mess up God's perfect design, your not-so-perfect people are going to mess up your "perfect" design also! So relax, because the quest for perfection will kill the desire for hospitality!

God and Hospitality

Hospitality is providing certain things for those in your environment. Such as:

- Food and other physical needs
- Fellowship
- Atmosphere
- Freedom and forgiveness (allowing people to make mistakes)
- Graciousness

When Jesus was on this earth He was a gracious hospitable person. He provided for those around Him. When someone had a need, Jesus took care of it.

Jesus provided food and other physical needs:

1. He changed water into wine
2. Broke bread for 5,000 people
3. He gave sight to a blind man

Jesus provided fellowship: Jesus says, "I am the bread of life. He who comes to me will never go hungry, and he who believes in me will never be thirsty" (John 6:35). He provided for their emotional needs by allowing them access to who is was.

Jesus provided atmosphere: He took the role of a servant and washed the disciple's feet. He was the host for the "Last

Supper." He created a welcoming atmosphere by being a servant to those in His presence.

Jesus provided free-will and forgiveness: The woman at the well was not living the life she should and was not accepted in her culture. Jesus allowed her to make mistakes and still forgave her of her wrong doing. He did not turn His back on her the way the rest of the town did.

Jesus provided graciousness: He made a woman caught in sin feel welcome in his presence when others wanted her to be condemned. He took care of people's physical, spiritual, and emotional needs. Jesus was a gracious host.

The very persona of God is that of a welcoming Creator. He created a garden—a home for the first man and woman. By His creation, God was and is saying, "Here I Am! I want you to see Me!"

Romans 1:20 says, "For since the creation of the world God's invisible qualities—his eternal power and divine nature—have been clearly seen, being understood from what has been made, so that men are without excuse." And after each day of creation God proclaimed that each thing He made was "Good." The reason each thing He makes is good, is because HE is good!

Psalm 145:9 says, "The Lord is good to all: he has compassion on all he has made."

Psalm 34:8a says, "Taste and see that the Lord is good."

And James 1:17 says, "Every good and perfect gift is from above, coming down from the Father of the heavenly lights . . ."

Even after Adam and Eve "messed-up" God's perfect plan, it did not change His love for them. Psalm 147:5b, "His understanding has no limit." What a gracious, hospitable God we have! But one of the reasons He created mankind in the first place was for the purpose of having a relationship with us. "I no longer call you servants, because a servant does not know his master's business. Instead, I have called you friends ..." John 15:15-16.

After mankind made a bad choice, God provided them with a way of escape. As hosts and hostesses one of the most comforting gifts you can give someone who enters your home is allowing them to make a mistake, and giving them a way out. God did this for us. He gave us His Son, and provided a way for us to always be able to associate with Him. If you believe God sent Jesus to die on the cross for the wrong things you have done, and if you believe that God raised Jesus from the grave, then God's Word says you are saved from an eternity in hell (Romans 10:9,10). If that is you – congratulations on taking God up on His eternal hospitality.

But there is more! God, our hospitable God, wants to give us more. After you have taken Him up on His offer of eternal life, John 16:24b says, "Ask and you will receive and your joy may be complete." God wants us to ask Him for whatever is in our hearts. He will provide what we need if we ask. Do you need encouragement? Do you need to be rescued from a bad situation? Do you need hope? Do you need security? Do you need endurance? God wants to provide for you, and He doesn't even expect you to be perfect! He is the picture of the most gracious hospitality. You are welcome in His world and He wants to provide for your needs. Are you hospitable? Do you have some things you need to overcome in order to be a gracious host?

Here are a couple of ways we can overcome our desire for perfection in order to be hospitable:

1. Try to remember what the house looks like after the party so that it doesn't seem quite as important to make everything perfect before the guests arrive.
2. Give your children specific things to pick up after the party. This will encourage you during the party that you will not have to do everything yourself.

These are practical examples but there is more to being hospitable than just having a good plan. We need to look at hospitality from a spiritual side.

Spiritual Thinking:

Hospitality is an attitude of the heart. This is the spiritual aspect of hospitality and the spiritual aspect of decorating.

Providing for those under your roof:

1. **Food and other physical needs**

   Most people have the easiest time with this aspect of hospitality. It is fairly simple to put food on the table. For some, this is not easy. If you worry about the amount of food or if it is adequate, have some people help you by bringing part or even most of the food. I usually have Christmas and Thanksgiving and Easter and the Fourth of July at my house. I love to decorate the table. I am not as good about fixing food. My theory is that as long as it is edible, it's fine. It is more important to me for the table to look good than for the food to taste good. I know that is not always the best thinking, and that is why I provide one or two items of food and I decorate the table. I have my guests bring the rest of the dinner. This works great for a couple of reasons. I get to do what I do best and my guests feel good about doing their part.

2. **Fellowship**

   As you think about the people you are going to invite, make sure they will enjoy one another's company. Although you will have much to do as a hostess, always make time for each of your guests: make eye contact, give them a hug, and let them know personally you are glad they were able to come.

3. **Atmosphere**

Plan your atmosphere. Pre-plan the music, the lighting and the fragrance that will be present in your home. Be prepared for those who may not be used to being around children. Have a special place for children to go if they were included in the invitation. If someone is having a hard time because of the noise level, do your best to meet their need. A good idea when having a party where a mixture of ages is represented is to have an in-house babysitter. Hire a teenager to be in charge of the kid area. Let them know what the house rules are for eating and drinking in the play area and that they can get extra snacks for the kids when the need arises. Allow them to do most of the damage control for the kids. Keep in mind the fact that they will not do it exactly the same as you.

4. **Freedom and forgiveness**

God gave mankind the choice to do right or wrong. There will be times when your guests choose to do something you did not want them to do. If you have freedom and forgiveness in place in your mind and heart – there will be a better outcome than if you show up at your own party unprepared. There are times when people break things, use things you didn't want them to use, go where you didn't want them to go, eat things they were not supposed to eat and when it is all said and done, they are not even sorry about it! Whew! That is irritating! Prepare your mind before they get to your house to have a forgiving attitude. Put away anything that is just not worth the risk and pray that God will help you to respond the way you should. When something does not go as planned, most of the time it is a bigger deal to us than it is to anyone else. We are usually the only one to notice. If we respond in anger, then everyone will notice. So take your anger to God and ask Him for help to respond outwardly the way you should.

5. Graciousness

Graciousness is the centerpiece of hospitality. It is the ability to make everyone comfortable emotionally, spiritually, and physically all at the same time. You cannot do this by yourself. You will be a gracious hostess if you keep in mind the things we have discussed in this book—things such as the fruit of the Spirit and letting go of perfectionism. When you can put fear and perfection on the shelf and let God be in you the way He desires – you are going to meet the needs you are supposed to and He will do what you cannot.

Design and Spiritual Homework

Here is the application: Get going! Don't just stand there, do something! It's time to put all that spiritual learning and improvement into action. This involves letting other people into your life.

Invite someone over. Maybe it is just a girlfriend for coffee or a family for dinner. It could be a couple for a small dinner party, but whatever it is – just do it! Most importantly, don't forget your neighbors and those who may not know the One who says to be hospitable. Invite them over so you can introduce them to the Designer who is helping you to be a very friendly, hospitable host!

CHAPTER NINE RECIPE: EASY RECIPES FOR COMPANY

Jana's Crock-pot Chili

1. Brown 1-2 lbs of ground beef
2. Put the cooked meat into the crock-pot
3. Add a large can of diced tomatoes
4. Also add a can of Rotel diced tomatoes and chilies
5. One can of chili beans
6. One can of water
7. One packet of chili seasoning
8. Put in 2-3 Tbsp of sugar
9. 1-2 Tbsp of red wine vinegar.

Put crock-pot on low if you are able to let it simmer for about 5 hrs. Put it on high if you need it to be done in 2 hrs. Serve chili with sour cream, shredded cheddar cheese, and frito chips. This makes a full crock-pot of chili.

All Day Chicken Soup (that takes ten minutes to put together)

1. Cut up 3 large scrubbed potatoes and put in crock-pot.
2. Put 3-4 boneless chicken breasts on top of potatoes.
3. Add two cans of cream of chicken soup.
4. Add a couple of spoonfuls of sour cream.
5. Add one package of ranch dressing powder.
6. Boil 1-2 cups of pasta (elbow, spiral). Toss these to the mixture before serving.
7. Salt and Pepper to taste.
8. Serve with shredded cheddar cheese.

You will want to let this cook for 2-3 hours on high or 4-5 hours on low. Make sure to cut through the chicken to make sure it has cooked all the way through. This makes 6-10 servings. You can also serve these in bread bowls.

Easy Chicken Enchiladas

1. 3-4 boneless Chicken Breasts (you can put these in frozen if you want) in crock-pot
2. 2 cans of cream of chicken or cream of mushroom soup. Or one of each.
3. 2 Tbsp sour cream
4. One can of Rotel diced tomatoes and chilies

Let cook in crock-pot 3-6 hrs depending on whether you have it on high or on low. Check the chicken to make sure that it is cooked all the way through.

Take the chicken pieces out of the crock-pot and cut into bite size pieces. Put into the larger size flour tortillas. Top with cheese and wrap laying them in a pam-sprayed baking dish. Keep cutting chicken and putting into tortillas, wrapping and laying them in the baking dish until you have used all the chicken or filled up the baking dish. Make sure they are laid side-by-side and not on top of each other. Then take any remaining pieces of chicken and scatter on top of the rolled enchiladas. Pour the remainder of the juices from the crock-pot over the rolled enchiladas. Top with cheddar cheese and bake in 350 degree oven for 10-15 minutes or until cheese is melted. This usually makes 1 9X13 pan plus 1 9x9 pan. It makes quite a bit and if you want it to go further, just throw in one or two more chicken breast pieces. I usually plan 1-1.5 enchiladas per person and serve rice and corn as side dishes.

Ivy's Homemade Salsa

4-5 cucumbers peeled and diced
6 Roma tomatoes diced
½ green bell pepper cleaned out and diced
½ red bell pepper cleaned out and diced
1 fresh chili pepper diced (be careful cutting these with your
      bare hands - the juice can cause burning - especially
      on dry hands)
1 bunch fresh cilantro
1 lime cut in half and squeezed into salsa
1-2 tablespoons sugar
sprinkle "Accent" flavor enhancer over the mixture

The above recipe is how I make it, but if you must – you can add an avocado and/or an onion. Serve with tortillas - I especially enjoy the lime flavored Tostitos.

Idea for keeping recipes: use a photo folder for 3x4 or 3x5 pictures to put your recipes in. These work great because they also protect against food damage.

These last four recipes are from my kitchen and I have a lot of fun with them. I thought however, it might be nice to have some recipes from an actual chef - I asked Kevin Barko the chef from our church if he would be so kind and share some of his recipes with me to share in turn with you. They look really good! Thanks Kevin.

Olive Oil Blessing
Christ Church of the Valley
Chef Kevin Barko

Baste grilled vegetables, toss with salad greens and croutons, brush on bread and pizza.

Yield: 1 ¼ Cups

2 garlic gloves, peeled
1 cup olive oil
3 tablespoons dried basil
2 tablespoons dried oregano
½ teaspoon kosher salt

In a blender, emulsify garlic and olive oil. Add spices, then turn blender on and off intermittently to mix thoroughly.

Store covered at room temperature until ready to use. The "blessing" will keep for about one week.

Raspberry-Maple Dressing
Christ Church of the Valley
Chef Kevin Barko

1 cup white wine vinegar
1 cup red wine vinegar
½ cup raspberries-fresh
½ cup olive oil
½ cup vegetable oil
¾ cup maple syrup
2 tablespoons Dijon mustard
2 tablespoons died tarragon leaves
Salt to taste

Prepare a raspberry vinegar
Combine red and white wine vinegars and raspberries. Cover and let sit for 4-8 hours. Strain and store at room temperature.

Whisk together a ½ cup of the raspberry vinegar, the oils, maple syrup, mustard, tarragon, and salt.

Whole Wheat Pita Bread
Christ Church of the Valley
Chef Kevin Barko

The Sponge
¾ cup warm water 110-115 degrees
5 teaspoons of active dry yeast
1 cup whole wheat flour

The Bread
1 ½ cups warm water
3 ½ cups whole wheat flour
½ cup vital wheat gluten
2 ½ tablespoons vegetable oil
1/3 cup honey
1 tablespoon salt

Making the sponge
Mix the warm water and yeast in your mixing bowl. Stir together and cover. Let sit for 45 minutes to one hour. When the sponge is ready uncover the bowl and continue to make your bread.

The Bread
Add 1 ½ cups of warm water and 2 cups of whole wheat flour – mix well. Add ½ cup vital wheat gluten, 2 ½ tablespoons salt – mix well. Add the remaining flour ½ cup at a time. Work the dough, approximately 10 minutes in the mixer or if you are kneading by hand 30-40 minutes. Form the dough into a ball and place into a greased bowl and let rise covered for 1 hour to

1 ½ hours until double in size. Now punch down and shape the dough into small 1 ½ inch balls. Place onto baking sheet and cover to raise again for about an hour. Turn your oven on 450. After bread has had a second raising roll out to a 10' round pita size. Bake on a cookie sheet for about 10 minutes until brown.

Serve with fresh greens or your favorite meal.

PART THREE

The Creator of Design

Psalm 68: 19-20a says, "Praise be to the Lord, to God our Savior, who daily bears our burdens. Our God is a God who saves."

Chapter ~ 10

THE ROOM WHERE YOU LIVE

Check-out time is 10 a.m. The price of the room is $200.00 for occupancy of up to four persons per night. In case of emergency call the 'Operator.' In case of fire feel the door to see if it is hot. If it is not hot, open it carefully and move keeping yourself as close to the ground as possible. For your security safety deposit boxes are available in the lobby."

This sign was on the inside of our hotel room when our family went on vacation in California. It is similar to signs I have seen in other hotel rooms around the country. I do not have one of those signs in my house because I live there and I get to make the rules for my home. The hotel has to post these signs because the people who stay in these rooms do not live there – they are only visiting. So let me ask you – where do you live? Where is the room that belongs to you? You may answer, Iowa or Minnesota, or Texas, but that is not really the room where you live. The room where you truly live has no windows or doors. It has no need for fabric or hardware, and no one can even be invited into this room except for One. So what will you use in the decorating of your heart, for this is truly where you

177

live? And if you know Jesus as your Savior, He is living there also. So let me ask you, is your guest comfortable in the spiritual room of your life, or is a renovation in order? Like other rooms, if you do not like the present décor, you can change it! That is the good news, but where should you start?

DECORATING YOUR HEART

First Floor – Décor

Ephesians 1:17-23 has a good place to start when it comes to the decorating of your heart. It shares three elements which make excellent accessories for your spiritual life.

> I keep asking that the God of our Lord Jesus Christ, the glorious Father, may give you the Spirit of wisdom and revelation, so that you may know him better. I pray also that the eyes of your heart may be enlightened in order that you may know the hope to which he has called you, the riches of his glorious inheritance in the saints, and his incomparably great power for us who believe. That power is like the working of his mighty strength, which he exerted in Christ when he raised him from the dead and seated him at his right hand in the heavenly realms, far about all rule and authority, power and dominion, and every title that can be given, not only in the present age but also in the one to come. And God placed all things under his feet and appointed him to be head over everything for the church, which is his body, the fullness of him who fills everything in every way.

Three elements to decorate your heart:

1. **The hope to which He has called you.** God has given us a hope – we can have eternal life through Jesus Christ

His Son. You have hope. He picked you and has a special plan for your life both in this present one and in the one to come.

2. **The riches of His glorious inheritance in the Saints.** This is your prestigious position because of your link to God as one of the saints.

3. **His incomparably great power for us who believe.** The Bible goes on to tell us that God has given us access to the same power that He used to raise Christ from the dead! At our disposal is the awesome power of God for our daily lives.

ACCESSORIZING YOUR SPIRIT

Second Floor – Accessories

There is another area of our spiritual lives that needs attention. How will you be accessorizing your Soul? Here are three must haves to start with in this area:

1. Wisdom – "Let the wise listen and add to their learning, and let the discerning get guidance" (Proverbs 1:5).

2. Discernment – "The man without the Spirit does not accept the things that come from the Spirit of God, for they are foolishness to him, and he cannot understand them, because they are spiritually discerned. The spiritual man makes judgments about all things, but he himself is not subject to any man's judgment; 'For who has known the mind of the Lord that he may instruct him?' But we have the mind of Christ" (I Corinthians 2:14-16).

3. Praise/Scripture – "Your Word is a lamp to my feet and a light for my path" (Psalm 119:105).

Let's take a closer look at how we can apply these into our lives.

Could I Have Mine With a Side Order of Wisdom Please!

When I was in high school one of my friends actually believed our youth pastor when he told her they had to turn Niagara Falls off at night to conserve energy. Wisdom is one of life's necessities that is sometimes found missing. Proverbs 1:5 says, "Let the wise listen and add to their learning. . ." King Solomon says to keep learning, and he should know. God made him the wisest man to ever live.

The whole book of Proverbs is devoted to wisdom. How does one become wise? Proverbs 1:7 says that the fear of the Lord is the beginning of knowledge. And in James 1:5 the Bible says that we can simply ask for it! How easy could that be? It even goes on to say that you will not frustrate God no matter how many times you ask for wisdom, but that He will give it to you generously! So what are we waiting for? Ask and keep asking!

There are times, though, where we should have known better, but made a bad decision. How does this happen? What is it that keeps us from using wisdom in our lives? "The wise woman builds her house, but with her own hands the foolish one tears hers down" (Proverbs 14:1).

The opposite of wisdom is foolishness. Foolishness creeps in the back door of our lives almost undetected. Then it springs to life in a moment of our natural self-passion and we look very much like the woman in Proverbs 14:1. As women, we really do believe we are right most of the time, and this is usually our biggest downfall. "Trust in the Lord with all your heart and lean not on your own understanding. In all thy ways acknowledge Him and He will make your paths straight" (Proverbs 3:5,6). When we think we're right, why would we ask for directions? And if we think we're right most of the time, how much of the time are we asking for God's wisdom? If we're honest with ourselves about this question the answer would be – almost none! Women might not mind asking for traffic directions, but on the home-front and in our own lives – whoa baby, watch out! The cool thing about this wisdom thing is that you can make a real mess of things but with one sentence of humility, it can be fixed, "God, I need your wisdom and I need it right now because I leaned on my own wisdom and have made a mess of things – help!"

Did you know that wisdom is not only something to learn, but wisdom can actually *enter* your heart? Proverbs 2:10 says, "For wisdom will enter your heart, and knowledge will be pleasant to your soul."

Proverbs 3:1-2 says, "But keep my commands in your heart for they will prolong your life many years and bring you prosperity."

Let's look at the four things we have learned about wisdom so far:

1. God will never get tired of us asking for wisdom.
2. Wisdom can enter your heart.
3. Wisdom can be kept.
4. Wisdom will bring you prosperity and a long life.

Another cool thing about God's wisdom is that He doesn't even care how you use it. Today I was with my family at Knott's Berry Farm and my twelve-year-old had two stuffed animals she was trying to decide between purchasing. She wanted me to make the decision for her. I told her she needed to make the decision but that she could ask God which would be the better choice and He would help her. She came back in a few moments with a smile on her face and a firm decision on which one to buy. Isn't it great that God cares about a twelve-year-old's decision to buy a stuffed animal! Think about the application of this to so many areas of our lives!

People frequently ask for prayer – sometimes the prayer is for their personal life, but most of the time it is for other people. Usually it is for other people with an illness or physical problem. We have prayer chains, prayer meetings, and prayer seminars. A whole bunch of books has been written on the subject of prayer. The concept of prayer is as vast as the character of the Author of prayer. It is so big and wonderful that I did not really want to venture into the subject, but the Holy Spirit compels me to say just a couple of things on the matter. First of all, prayer is for everyone. You may not think you have met up to a certain standard of quality needed to make this a habit in your life, but God is not looking for perfection in order to listen to you. "The Lord is near to all who call on him," (Psalm 145:18). Perhaps you have been a believer most of your life and this concept of prayer is not new to you. After all, prayer is just talking to God. Some of us learned this when we were still in diapers.

But I have been noticing something for the past couple of years that just kind of bothers me. Someone will have a prayer request and they will call me and say, "Pray – pray hard and long that God will ..." Then they will add, "Get as many people as you can to pray for this. We already have several churches bathing this matter in prayer." Now that sounds really spiritual. But one question would always come to my mind. Don't they believe God when He says, "You may ask me for anything in my name, and I will do it" (John 14:14). I don't mean to take away from all the Scriptures about prayer – there are many passages about prayer. But I'm not sure God ever meant it to be so complicated. Sometimes when people have these big prayer chains on someone's behalf it almost sounds like they are trying to qualify to get a "yes" answer from God. Even among the godliest people there is this unstated belief that if we get enough people praying long and hard enough then God will change His mind. I don't believe this is a biblical view on prayer, when we take the scripture as a whole thought. There are passages that say we can call God our "Abba" father, and the Bible says we may boldly enter into the throne room of God. Other passages say that God has our hairs numbered, and He keeps a record of our tears in a bottle. This does not sound like the prayer counting, arm folding God that only answers "yes" to prayers that have been labored over. Paul says, "After beginning with the Spirit, are you now trying to attain your goal by human effort," (Gal. 3:3). If we are not careful, we turn prayer into something we can accomplish with our own human effort!

I do believe God wants us to pray together and in large groups, but I do not think that it is for the same reasons most Christians practice praying this way. The more people who are involved in praying for something specific – the more people God is able to bless with His answer! Why waste a perfectly good miracle on only one or two people when a whole bunch of people can be blessed and give God the glory? Definitely ask people to join in your prayer, but remember that even answers to prayer are for God's glory and not our own.

Can I Get Some Discernment on the Side, or Will That Cost Extra?

The second necessity to include is discernment. Discernment is one of the most unglamorous virtues on which to think. It goes pretty much unnoticed unless it is missing completely and it is about as much fun as spending Christmas money on socks. But it is necessary! There are a couple of different aspects of discernment to inspect. First of all is the area of discerning God's will, wisdom, or spirit as opposed to our will, wisdom or other spirits. Have you ever felt confusion when making a decision? This is when discernment becomes extremely important for our lives and those we are responsible to bring up. If we start with wisdom, other things in life seem to fall into place. I Corinthians 2:4-5 says, "My message and my preaching were not with wise and persuasive words, but with a demonstration of the Spirit's power, so that your faith might not rest on men's wisdom, but on God's power."

Praise and Scripture to Go!

The last essential we will consider is the area of praise and Scripture reading. Well of course Scripture reading is important, but how important is praise? Usually you will hear someone talk about prayer and Bible reading, but praise? Frequently when we pray it sounds more like a wish list for the sick in our families. We should pray for the sick, but the true heart of prayer is first of all praise filled. God wants to hear us praise Him. The person who praises God often will have a glass half full attitude in life rather than a glass half empty. When we remember who God is and what He has done for us – it makes us thankful. Then we can add to that praise a time of thanksgiving. After we're done with all that praising and thanksgiving it is kind of hard to have a bad attitude or be filled with fear. Praise is an essential in our spiritual decorating kit! Psalm 89:1-2 says, "I will sing of the Lord's great love forever; with my mouth I will make your faithfulness known through all generations. I will declare that your love stands firm forever, that you established your faithfulness in heaven itself."

ORGANIZING YOUR MIND

Third Floor – Organization

Everything in life is about containers. For instance: the bookcase contains books. The books contain chapters. The chapters contain words. The words contain thoughts. The thoughts contain emotion. Emotions contain the essence of God, of which we are made up. We are made in the image of God, thus relating us to the things in our lives. There are intangible things that cannot always be broken down in this container way, but almost every tangible thing can be related to containers. A purse contains the things I need to carry with me. A car contains me on my way to doing the various and sundry things in life. My home contains my possessions. My computer contains these and other words I have written, and on and on the list goes. Years contain months, months contain weeks, weeks contain days, and days contain hours, which contain minutes, which contain seconds. God made time for us – time does not contain God.

In this entire contained world God is teaching us about Himself. Our hearts are to be a container – of His wisdom, His love, and His unselfishness. Our hearts are to be containers of Him, and like containers, not all are the same. They come in all shapes and sizes. They are made up of plastic, wood, and any number of other materials. He wants us to be completed by Him while abiding in Him or becoming contained by Him. John 15:3-5 says, "You are already clean because of the work I have spoken to you. No branch can bear fruit by itself; it must remain in the vine. Neither can you bear fruit unless you remain in me. 'I am the vine; you are the branches. If a man remains in me and I in him, he will bear much fruit; apart from me you can do nothing.'" Paul called it being a prisoner of Christ. With salvation I get the promised Holy Spirit who chooses to be confined or contained in me, and so the circle is complete. When I know Jesus as my Savior, He is living in me. When I am living the way God wants, I am abiding in Him – contained! Not only am I contained, but also content because I am secure in God. It's a nice place to be!

COLORIZING YOUR SPIRIT

Fourth Floor – Color Coordinates

God is your internal decorator. Let him colorize you from the inside using His fruit. *"But the fruit of the Spirit is love, joy, peace, patience, kindness, goodness, faithfulness, gentleness and self-control.,"* (Gal 5:22-23). Sometimes it is easy to scrutinize what is wrong and forget to exercise what is good and useful. In these verses God tells us what our focus should be for life. There is something else about Jesus that we need to add to our lives. His *passion*!

The smell of freshly popped popcorn lingering in the air was almost enough to draw her away from the game, but not quite. She couldn't pull herself away – the uniforms, what beautiful colors. The team looked so sharp – and those shoes! Oh, to wear those someday! Although she was only seven years old, she had already made up her mind – one day she would be on that team. It seemed like such a long way off. Would it ever arrive? Would she ever be in high school, and if so, would she make the team? Of all the sports a little girl dreams of I believe cheerleading has to be at the top of the list. Along with cheerleading as an ambition in life there are also – nurses, mommies, firemen, teachers, and racecar drivers. These are all common answers to the question – what do you want to be when you grow up? I happen to know that the little girl who dreamed of becoming a cheerleader found her desire fulfilled.

What makes the difference between a person who succeeds and one who only dreams? When do you cross the line from an idea to reality? What is the difference between someone who is merely saved and someone who is saved and living the wonderful Holy Spirit led life? I believe the answer to all these questions can be summed up in one word – passion.

When I was sitting in the stands at a basketball game quite a few years ago now, I was not watching the ball game. My eyes were fixed on the cheerleaders. If I shut my eyes I can still see them today even though I have seen many cheerleading squads since then. In me was born an insatiable desire to be part of the cheerleading squad. When I was old enough to learn some of the moves and gymnastics, I worked on it all the time. Why? Because I had a bigger picture in mind. I could already see my-self in the uniform with the matching shoes. I had a passion that would overcome any obstacles I found myself up against because I just *had* to be on a cheerleading squad. I was willing to go through physical pain or difficulty, embarrassment, fatigue, ridicule, and whatever else it might take to be on that squad. I was even willing to go through the pain of rejection, because of course, you have to try out. Do you think I made the team? You bet! Now there were many other things I attempted and did not succeed. I was not as passionate about them.

On our cheerleading team there were no alternates. There were simply – the cheerleaders. No one sat out. In basketball you have first line, second line, benchwarmers, water-boys, team managers, assistant coaches etc. It is conceivable one could go out for this type of sport, and sit on the bench all year not making one difference in the outcome of that team's year. For some it is enough to simply make the team. For others, once they make the team, they have the drive and determination to move up by improving their game. There is a passion for the sport, for the team, or school for which they are playing.

I have a friend who played on the team for which I cheered. He was just as passionate about playing and winning as I was about cheering for him and the other players. He went on to become coach of that team and is still the coach today, as far as I know. His brother told me he bought a satellite so that he could have over 200 channels of just sports. He watches the game continually so that he can improve the game because he is passionate about it.

The person who is content to sit on the sidelines or even sit in the stands is not passionate about the sport. The parents watching from the stands are passionate about seeing their child play. Just as there are different viewpoints in a basketball game there are different viewpoints in the Christian walk. The difference between just being content to be on the team, and being the one who shoots the winning score is passion.

The Bible brings up these different viewpoints in several places. I really believe this passion is what makes all the difference in the world. There are Christians who are just glad they're not going to hell. There are those who are glad they're on the team and will help out when asked, but hope no one asks them to help. There are those who help out the "ministry" thinking somehow this will win them brownie points with God. (They don't get how the game is played because they didn't read the rule book.) There are those who get the big picture in life, and have a heart of passion for what God wants them to accomplish. These people go after their passion like a star athlete.

When you let God glorify himself through you, your life will be more than you ever dreamed. As you *Save Perfection for Heaven* in the decorating of your home and enjoy using the five senses God gave you, my prayer for you is that your home will truly become a Work of Heart.

CHAPTER TEN RECIPE: THE ROOM WHERE YOU LIVE JOURNAL

Date:

Scripture:

Journal entry:

Prayer:

Date:

Scripture:

Journal entry:

Prayer:

Date:

Scripture:

Journal entry:

Prayer:

Date:

Scripture:

Journal entry:

Prayer:

Date:

Scripture:

Journal entry:

Prayer:

Date:

Scripture:

Journal entry:

Prayer:

Psalm 73:23-24 says, "Yet I am always with you; you hold me by your right hand you guide me with your counsel and afterward you will take me to glory."

Chapter 11

A WORK OF HEART

Once there was a prince and he wanted to marry a princess, but she must be a real princess. He was an expert traveler, and had seen the entire world, and met lots of people, but he had not found a real princess. Many women claimed to be princesses and indeed they were, but he wanted a *real* princess. Some of the women he met wore exquisite gowns and expensive jewels in their crowns. Most of them could glide across the room in their ballroom dresses looking like they didn't even move their legs. They all knew when to curtsey and how to sit with an absolutely straight back. They smiled when appropriate, and remained solemn at correct intervals. Each had her own measure of grace, and a commanding presence filled the room when one of them entered. But he felt something was missing and returned home feeling rather sad, for he had not found a real princess, and was beginning to doubt whether such a person existed.

One night there was a terrible storm, which started many fires across the countryside. The villagers were forced out of their homes and scattered near and far wondering how they would rebuild their dwellings and where their families would live in the meantime.

But the castle of the prince was unharmed and quite warm. They were rejoicing in their good fortune when they heard a knock on the big castle door. Very curious as to who might be at the door in the middle of such a night, the prince himself answered the door.

Standing before him was a young woman. She may have been a beautiful young woman, but he couldn't tell, for she was wearing torn and soiled clothing and had smudges on her face and hands. They stood looking at each other for an awkward moment, and then the woman spoke, "I'm sorry to intrude at such an hour, but I am the Princess of the country next to yours and we have been burned out of our homes, and my people are scattered abroad. I have no place to go and was hoping I might spend the night."

"I-I'm sorry," stammered the prince for he had been taking all of this in and the one question that plagued his mind hindered him from keeping up with the conversation. "Won't you come in, and, of course, you may spend the night."

"Thank you for your kindness," answered the woman, stifling a yawn, for she was very tired.

The prince's mother, who had observed all this from the other side of the room, approached. "You must be very tired after all you have been through! I will prepare a room for you."

"You are too kind," replied the young woman following the queen to her room.

While the young woman bathed, the queen prepared a bed for her. Determined to find out for her son whether this be a true princess or not, she ordered the maids to pile twenty mattresses on the guest's bed. Then she took a pea, just a dried up old pea and put it under the bottom mattress. "There," she smiled to herself, "We shall see if a true princess you are!"

The next morning at breakfast the prince asked the young woman if she had enjoyed a good night of sleep. "I'm afraid I didn't sleep much at all!" replied the guest.

"Why not?" asked the queen. "Was there something wrong with your bed?"

"I don't know," said the girl. "How could I indulge myself with a comfortable bed when my villagers are scattered abroad with no homes to return to – I slept on the floor."

"My son," said the queen, "I believe you have found a true princess!"

A true princess will reveal herself by her actions. If you know Jesus as your Savior you are a real princess. But do your actions betray or prove your title?

After all is said and done, what should be our true motive in decorating? We have answered the questions as to why we are inclined to decorate, but why *should* we decorate? The majority of people would say: because it feels good, we want to, we have the talent to, or we want to impress people with our homes. But if imitation is the greatest form of flattery, what does this say about our ultimate reason behind the creation of our designs? Whether we are believers in a Creator or not, we are creatures following after their Master Designer with an inward desire to do as He did – create, design, and decorate whatever we can. Whether we believe He exists or not, we imitate Him. Every time we decorate we are mimicking what happened during the first days the earth existed. So truly decorating is impersonating God in a small way. But should it be more? Is decorating supposed to be more than just a good counterfeit job? Is God looking for it to be more? Is decorating, in fact, supposed to be an act of worshiping the One who came up with the idea in the first place? Or, if not, could it be turned into one?

The definition of "Worship" as stated by Merriam-Webster is as follows: "Reverence offered a divine being or supernatural power, also: an act of expressing such reverence."[1]

Notice the "*Act* of expressing such reverence" part of the definition? In worship we usually think of people lifting their hands in worship, kneeling, taking communion, or simply praying. While all of these are good forms of worship, are we limited to only these?

Acts of Worship

In the Old Testament Abraham built altars to make sacrifices to God as an act of worship (Gen. 22). Abraham's grandson, Enos, was compelled to give a part of the product of their labor as an act of worship. The Old Testament is filled with examples of acts of worship. During the times of sacrifice, there were a lot of different kinds of offerings made with the understanding that this was done out of reverence for the Creator. Reverence, according to Webster, is, "Honor or respect felt or shown, profound adoring, awed respect, or a gesture of respect."[1] It is interesting that it is not enough to simply feel respect but that we must act upon that feeling. And when we do this it is called – worship.

There were numerous ceremonies occupying the Jewish life during Old Testament times and these also were acts of worship to the One they served. All of these acts of worship and even acts of worship we use today, are all outward expressions of our inward feelings toward God – the Creator. When Jesus was on earth people marveled at his miracles. Luke 9:37-45 is one such account. Jesus cast a demon out of a young boy, and the Bible says that "They were amazed at the majesty of God." I find it interesting that this miracle Jesus performed was the subtraction of something evil rather than just the addition of something glorious. The people were amazed at the total lack of evil which they had become accustomed to in the boy. Evil is so primal to our being that we cannot imagine a world without it. When we catch a glimpse of the purity of life as it is supposed to be, it leaves us in awe. Remember – awe is part of worship.

David said, in Psalm 29: 2b, "Worship the Lord in the beauty of holiness" (KJV). It is interesting that God puts together in one verse, beauty and worship and holiness. Why do these three belong together? We have discussed the definition of worship and holiness is the subtraction of evil, so what exactly does the Bible mean by beauty of holiness?

In the Hebrew the word beauty is translated "Hadarah." It occurs five times in the Old Testament and means "to adorn" or "decorate!" So I reread the verse to say something like, worship the Lord in the decoration of His holiness. Holiness is God's favorite accessory! It is His defining quality. It is what He wants to be known for, and David understood that there is nothing as beautiful as the absence of evil! Every time I subtract evil from my life I am putting on the holiness that God enjoys. It is not only the addition factor we need to remember in having God as part of our lives, but the subtraction of evil.

II Corinthians 7:1 ties things up neatly, "Since we have these promises, dear friends, let us purify ourselves from everything that contaminates body and spirit, perfecting holiness out of reverence for God." Wow! Ok, that just took our whole book and put it into one basic sentence, because it is not our homes we are to be perfecting, but our inward being. We are subtracting evil and perfecting our lives out of reverence for God!

So, can decorating be an act of worship? Well - worship is admiration, adoration, and respect for God. Therefore we conclude that an act of worship can be any outward expression or symbol of our admiration toward the Creator, even imitating His design! So the answer to the question, "Can decorating be an act of worship" is - it already is an act of worship! But what are we worshiping?

Romans 1:25 says, "They exchanged the truth of God for a lie, and worshiped and served created things rather than the Creator – who is forever praised. Amen." In America today, if we are not careful, we are idolaters of interior design. We become so enamored with our own or other's abilities that we forget the Ultimate Designer. Just as a singer can sing without giving glory to God, and a preacher can preach without giving glory to God, so can a designer create without giving God credit. But with a conscious decision even decorating can be put into perspective and made into the act of worship it is. We just need to add the heart behind the action realizing what we are doing. That was our early Bible application for this chapter. But we still have more to include about God's decorating/creation plan. How does the subject of worship relate to decorating our homes and does God want to be known for His creation of the world?

Psalm 19:1-6

> The heavens declare the glory of God; the skies proclaim the work of his hands. Day after day they pour forth speech; night after night they display knowledge. There is no speech or language where their voice is not heard. Their voice goes out into all the earth, their words to the ends of the world. In the heavens he has pitched a tent for the sun, which is like a bridegroom coming forth from his pavilion, like a champion rejoicing to run his course. It rises at one end of the heavens and makes its circuit to the other; nothing is hidden from its heat.

God's Word says that His glory has been proclaimed by the creation He has made! This Psalm says that the skies proclaim the very work of His hands. All people see what He has made in every country and in every language – nature is shouting the majesty of God. The word "knowledge" in verse 2 is translated "Knowledge that is gained through the senses!" This form of the word knowledge appears in the Old Testament 93 times!

Romans 1:20 says, "For since the creation of the world God's invisible qualities – his eternal power and divine nature- have been clearly seen, being understood from what has been made, so that men are without excuse." So all mankind has been shown the glory of God. Rich or poor, old and young all have been shown in a way that is understood by all to be God's handiwork.

I Chronicles 16:29 says, "Give unto the Lord the glory due unto his name..." (KJV). So what happens if we fail to obey this command? There is a warning about beauty, for beauty is something that God can cast down. Lamentations 2:1 says, "How the Lord has covered the Daughter of Zion with the cloud of his anger! He has hurled down the splendor of Israel from heaven to earth."

In Isaiah 44:13 the prophet Isaiah writes about a man making an image to worship the work of his own hands. Sometimes we build things according to our own idea of beauty – and admire too closely the work of our own hands. Isaiah 23:9 and 28:1-4 tell about Jehovah destroying all beauty which has its own source. In Ezekiel 16 God warns Jerusalem who trusted in its own beauty instead of giving God glory for what He had done. Ezekiel 31 and 32 tell about people lifting up their own works and their own beauty instead of God's and He speaks about bringing them down because of it.

So, does God want credit for what He has created? I believe we can safely say – Yes! Not only does He want it, He requires it! If you had been responsible for a work of art wouldn't you want credit for it? In the same way, we are called to worship Him as the Creator. God's beauty is far more complex than our beauty. It is so complex that He actually equipped us with five senses to take in the beauty He created. He made up the whole concept of beauty. He is beauty!

We should look for a moment at the difference between beauty and beautiful.

Beauty is the quality in a person or thing that gives pleasure to the senses. So, first of all, beauty is a quality. Secondly, beauty is a quality that gives pleasure. The only way for us to enjoy beauty is through the senses God gave us. So beauty is giving off pleasure to the senses. But beautiful according to Merriam-

Webster is, "Having qualities of beauty." So a beautiful person actually possesses beauty. Basically someone who is beautiful is someone who possesses the attributes of God, for He is beauty. I am speaking of actual, internal beauty, for there are some who outwardly possess qualities that are admired by anyone with the sense of seeing. But real beauty, inward and everlasting beauty, can only be collected by knowing God on a personal level.

My grandmother used to say "Pretty is as pretty does." When someone actually possesses beauty, then we say, "That is a beautiful person." If a person just gives off pleasure to the senses and has a quality of beauty she is not beautiful because she does not actually possess it. So, that's beauty, but what about all this, Save Perfection for Heaven? If I'm supposed to be saving perfection for heaven, what do I have to look forward to? Good question! Let's look at this place called Heaven.

This Place Called Heaven

First of all, there is an interesting group of items that will not be included in the celestial kingdom. The first and most obvious thing that will be missing is the presence of light, lamps, electricity, or sun, moon, and stars. Now from the decorating standpoint, that could be a problem! But there's more missing! There will also be no closing of the gate! There will be no unholy thing or person allowed to enter. And there will be no tears! Now what are we going to do? We're women, we like to cry! I thought you said it was going to be perfect! What's with all these missing things? Well, hold on, there are still more missing things. There will be no more death, mourning, or pain! Could there really be anything more precious than that? But wait a minute, there is something even more precious than that. One very important feature that *will* be present is Jesus! In fact, He is the very reason there is no need for any of the above. We are going to take a look at why His presence makes all the difference. Quite frankly I feel silly even trying to describe heaven, because it is technically indescribable. However, there is a lot to look forward to in eternity so let's look at what kind of **place** heaven is.

1. **Heaven is a place prepared by Jesus!** John 14:1-2, "Do not let your hearts be troubled. Trust in God; trust also in me. In my Father's house are many rooms; if it were not so, I would have told you. I am going there to prepare a place for you; I will come back and take you to be with me that you also may be where I am." Jesus is the Interior Designer of Heaven and He knows how to stimulate our five senses perfectly!

2. **Heaven is a place for seeing beauty.** In fact, heaven will be a place that possesses all beauty. Revelation 21:2, "I saw the Holy City, the new Jerusalem, coming down out of heaven from God, prepared as a bride beautifully dressed for her husband." What a great description, because of all the days in a woman's life, her wedding day is the day she strives to be the most beautiful. Sight is a necessary sense in order to enjoy Heaven. It is nice to know everyone will be able to enjoy the beautiful sights of eternity.

We said earlier there will be no light. Jesus *is* the light of heaven. His presence and glory illuminate the eternal dwelling (Rev. 21:23). He will always be present, which means there will be more things missing in Heaven. Darkness and night will be gone forever. The colors of heaven are the colors of twelve precious stones: jasper, sapphire, chalcedony, emerald, sardonyx, carnelian, chrysolite, beryl, topaz, chrysoprase, jacinth, and amethyst. The walls of the city are of jasper and the city of pure gold is as clear as glass. The main focal point will be the very throne of God! In Ezekiel's vision of heaven, he saw what looked like a throne of sapphire and an appearance of a man high above. "And brilliant light surrounded him. Like the appearance of a rainbow in the clouds on a rainy day, so was the radiance around him. This was the appearance of the likeness of the glory of the Lord. When I saw it, I fell facedown..." (Ezekiel 1:27a-28b). Is it possible that God himself is made up of all the colors?

As for the shapes and fabrics of heaven, Ezekiel saw wheels and he also described a man clothed in linen. Daniel refers to God as "Ancient of Days." In Daniel's vision of heaven he sees God's clothes as white as snow and His hair white like wool. He describes the throne as a flaming fire and its wheels are also on fire. But the most interesting "fabric" we are told about is found in Isaiah 6:1, "I saw the Lord seated on a throne, high and exalted, and the train of his robe filled the temple." Of all the things that there will be to look at in heaven, it is the glory of God that will overwhelm us – for we will actually get to see Jesus!

3. **Heaven is a place to feel alive and act in service:** I Timothy 4:8, "...but godliness has value for all things, holding promise for both the present life and the life to come." Also, the description of heaven in the book of Revelation is one that is full of life – it is not pictured as angels sitting on some cloud playing a harp! Revelation 22:3, "No longer will there be any curse. The throne of God and of the Lamb will be in the city, and his servants will serve him." So there will be acts of service to be done. The texture of heaven is amazing! Ezekiel, Daniel, Isaiah and John describe it in detail and it is still hard to put into words. Like we did in our chapter on

texture, let's look at the things these authors describe as part of heaven's texture: cherubim, wings, eyes, wheels, precious gems, seraphim, thrones, and glory, one creature with the face of lion and the face of eagle and the face of a man and the face of a bull. Some of us might be saying – "Hold on! That doesn't sound perfect, or pretty! What happened to all the rainbows and clouds and angels?" Remember, texture is about the element of surprise, the unexpected. Reading some of the passages about heaven makes me see that God will definitely have some texture going on that we were not prepared for! And guess what, God made heaven for men too! All the men are going to say, "Four-headed creatures – how cool is that!"

4. **Heaven is a place that sounds like worship:** Revelation 19:1a, "After this I heard what sounded like the roar of a great multitude in heaven shouting; 'Hallelujah!'" Let me tell you something, I just finished reading a bunch of verses on heaven looking for verbs about sound and you know what – heaven is going to be loud! Ezekiel 10:5 says, "The sound of the wings of cherubim could be heard as far away as the outer court, like the voice of the Almighty when He speaks." That's loud! Many times when Scripture refers to someone talking it says "In a loud voice." Revelation 4:5 speaks of peals of thunder around the throne. Revelation 4:8b says, "Day and night they never stop saying; 'Holy, holy, holy is the Lord God Almighty, who was, and is, and is to come.'"

There are other clues as to the sounds of heaven: they sang, the voice of many angels, rumblings, earthquakes, sounds of trumpets, and in a loud voice they sang. You thought you had a loud house! I am positive it doesn't even come close to the noise that will be part of heaven. For those of you who don't like loud music and noise, the good news is that it won't bother you because the important thing is that finally Jesus is going to be getting the praise He deserves and we get to be part of it! "Then I heard every creature in heaven, and on earth and under the earth and on the sea, and all that is in them, singing, 'To him who sits on the throne and to the Lamb be praise and honor and glory and power, for ever and ever!" (Rev. 5:13).

5. **Heaven is a place of glory or perfection:** II Corinthians 4:17, "For our light and momentary troubles are achieving for us an eternal glory that far outweighs them all." Finally, we get to talk about perfection! Ahh – here it is, the place where there will be no dirty underwear behind the bathroom door! No muddy footprints in the kitchen, nothing to get in our way, or hurt our feelings, no bad motives, or mistakes. There will be no dislikes, or disappointments or lack of funds to complete projects! That place we have been trying to get back to since the Garden of Eden is here and it is glorious and perfect. "For the wedding of the Lamb has come and his bride has made herself ready. The angel said to me, "Write; 'Blessed are those who are invited to the wedding supper of the Lamb!'" and he added, "these are the true words of God." At this I fell at his feet to worship him. But he said to me, "Do not do it! I am a fellow servant with you and with your brothers who hold to the testimony of Jesus. Worship God!" (Rev. 19:7b-10). Looking at all that perfection it would be easy to forget why we should look forward to heaven. It is not because of the perfection but because of the perfect One! We are going to worship Him!

6. **Heaven is Home!** When someone returns home for Christmas break one of the first things that makes them feel at home is the distinctive fragrance. So here's a question for you - how does heaven smell? "He was given much incense to offer, with the prayers of all the saints, on the golden altar before the throne. The smoke of the incense, together with the prayers of the saints, went up before God from the angel's hand" (Revelation 8:3-4).

There are several references to incense in heaven. Incense in heaven is always being offered along with prayer. Prayer is something that smells good to God. In the chapter on smelling, we referred to God decorating our survival kit - air and water! Our essentials for spiritual life are: Remember, refresh, and reflect. Don't forget to include things in décor that reflect, like water. In heaven there will be a river flowing from the throne, down the middle of the great street. Frank E. Gaebelein's Expositor's Bible Commentary says this of heaven's water source, "In both Testaments water is frequently associated with the salvation of God and the life-imparting and cleansing ministry of the Holy Spirit. In the new city of God the pure water does not issue from the temple as in Ezekiel but comes from the throne of God, since this whole city is a Most Holy Place with God at its center. Life from God streams unceasingly through the new world." God includes the refreshment of water in our eternal home.

And the last sense to bring into our heavenly home is that of taste. What will we eat in heaven? Well, according to Revelation 22:2 there will be the tree of life, bearing twelve crops of fruit, giving a different fruit every month.

Who knew? God belongs to the fruit of the month club! Besides wonderful smells and good food, home is a place of comfort and that is just what God has planned for heaven. God and His people will be united in heaven. He will wipe every tear from their eyes. There will be no more death or mourning or crying or pain. For the old order of things has passed away" (Revelation 21:3b-4). God goes on to say in verse 6-7, "It is done. I am the Alpha and the Omega, the Beginning and the End. To him who is thirsty I will give to drink without cost from the spring of the water of life. He who overcomes will inherit all this, and I will be his God and he will be my son." This is the comfort and belonging that is ours when we get to heaven with God our hospitable Father who offers food and drink. This is home!

Ever get tired down here? Do you ever long for a break, and for someone else to take over for you? Ever get tired of trying to keep it all going just the way it is supposed to? Do you need encouragement to enjoy your life and not feel like you have to keep reaching for this unattainable level of perfection? Relax, take the weight off your shoulders and put it on Him – He invites you to do this in I Peter 5:7. "Cast all your anxiety on him because he cares for you." or in other words, "Save Perfection for Heaven."

Ok, it's Heaven – but what do I wear!

She walks thoughtfully down each aisle running her hand through the folds of fabric, smelling the scent of garments ready to be formed. Six months left to plan, but it has taken a lifetime of preparation. An avid seamstress since high school, she has many years of experience, but this is such an important dress! She will need to give it much thought.

A Work of Heart

She comes to the final aisle feeling somewhat overwhelmed and a little discouraged having not yet found what she is looking for. This aisle is disheveled and takes some maneuvering to manage the looking. She pushes that bolt aside, and pulls this one feeling the texture of the fabric and trying to visualize what it will look like in the pattern she has had for years. Then, she sees something, just the corner of it sticking out from a pile of discarded bolts of fabric. The most beautiful cloth she has ever seen. She removes with great care the stack of fabrics until she uncovers the one she is looking for. It is perfect!

Carrying it gently through the aisles of unwanted material she comes to lay it on the cutting table. She is actually a little short of breath and her voice sounds far away as she says, "I will take twenty yards please."

The worker smiles a knowing look at her and reminds her to get the buttons, zipper, and thread which hang on the side wall. "Don't hesitate to ask for help if you need it," the clerk says tossing her words in the air as the girl is already on her way to find the appropriate color of thread. She will need at least five spools.

Having gathered all the necessary components she stands at the cash register ready to complete the purchase. The store is rather small, probably a family business, and she waits while the clerk comes from behind the cutting table to take her place as cashier.

"Ding! Ding!" rings the register as it tallies her bill. She's a little nervous knowing it will be the most expensive dress she has ever made. The clerk names the price, the check is written, and the girl leaves the shop for home, already planning the next phase of her little project.

It takes a lot of preparation to get to the actual sewing of a garment. You have to plan your pattern, shop for fabric, and figure out which way to lay out the pattern. That can take longer than sewing it.

So now you are finally ready to sew! Have you met the goal? Not by a long shot. You have taken a few things and prepared them to create into something beautiful. No short-cuts please. Don't leave it unfinished, don't get side-tracked. There will be mistakes along the way, but take the time to fix them. This dress must be perfect. Although you might enjoy sewing – sewing is not the goal. The ultimate goal is *wearing* the garment.

The dress we are speaking of is your wedding dress. Well, I'm already married you might be thinking, but our goal as Christians is to be the bride of Christ (Rev. 21:2).

Salvation is our engagement time. We are preparing for our wedding and our marriage. Picture your wedding dress. The bows will stand for longsuffering, the buttons for patience, the lace for purity, the hem for faith, the pearls will stand for each trial you came through victorious, the veil for holiness, the train for righteousness, and the headpiece for truth. What a beautiful picture of a bride! What man wouldn't want her!

But as you walk closer to your prince and He takes a better look at your dress, does He see that being tired one night you spilled coffee on the dress's train? (You didn't keep a clear conscience.) You cut the pattern too big and didn't bother to fix it, because you lacked patience. You left the hem undone because you were weary in doing good deeds, instead of remaining faithful. There were no pearls on your dress because you never let Him work through the trials in your life, you complained about them. Your veil was uneven and torn in places because you didn't take time to put truth into your life through times in God's Word and prayer. There is not enough lace because you lacked purity in your life, and the lace you have is yellow and faded.

No woman wants to look like this on her wedding day! How about you? You may be married and we have talked about being mentally one with your husband, but are you preparing for your Prince? Remember, you may not have married a prince, but you are engaged to one. Can you recall the excitement of the engagement time with the flurry of activity making sure everything was right? Remember longing to spend a few stolen moments together even if it were only to look into each other's eyes with hopefulness and anticipation? And you wanting to know everything he liked or disliked, wanting never to displease him, and wanting him to be proud of you.

When you received Jesus as your Savior, you said "yes." Jesus also said "yes." He said "Yes, I will take you right where you are, dirty lace and all." He accepts you with your past sins, your present sins, knowing you would probably choose to sin in the future. He hasn't called the wedding off. He still wants you. Therein is true intimacy. You are engaged. This is your preparation time!

But He, like any groom, still desires your best. He knows it will bring you true joy. Then one day when He comes back He can say, "See, I've completed you, you're perfect, thank you for being my friend on earth, thank you for following when I led, and for taking care of my business while I was away, well done." And you can say, "Thank you for being my Completer. Thank you for making *me* Perfect!"

BIBLIOGRAPHY

Blankenbaker, E. Keith. *Painting and Decorating: Skills and Techniques for Success.* Tinsley Park, Illinois: The Goodheart-Willcox Company, Inc., 2000.

Eiseman, Leatrice. *Colors for your Every Mood Discover Your True Decorating Colors.* Sterling, Virginia: Capital Books Inc., 2000.

Fletcher, Sir Banister. *A History of Architecture.* Nineteenth edition edited by John Musgrove. The Royal Institute of British Architects and the University of London, 1987.

Gaebelein, Frank E. *The Expositor's Bible Commentary.* Zondervan Publishing House 5th edition, 1981.

Ryan, Elaine. *Color Your Life!* ERA Publishing, 1987.

Smith, W. Stevenson, revised by William Kelly Simpson. *The Art and Architecture of Ancient Egypt.* World Print LTD., 1999.

Tan, Paul Lee. *Encyclopedia of 7700 Illustrations Signs of the Times.* Assurance Publishers, 1984.

Taylor, Lesley. *Inside Colour the Secrets of Interior Style.* New York: Sterling Publishing Co., 2000.

Tobias, Cynthia Ulrich. *The Way They Learn.* Tyndale House Publishers, 1994.

Trocme, Suzanne. *Influential Interiors shaping 20th century style through key interior designers.* Clarkson Potter; 1 Amer ed edition 1999.

Unger, Merrill F. Th.D., Ph.D. *Unger's Bible Dictionary.* Moody Press, 1982.

Wharton, Edith and Codman, Jr., Ogden. *The Decoration of Houses (Classical America Series in Art and Architecture).* New York: W.W Norton and Company, Inc., 1997.

Internet sites

Google search

http://homepages.ius.edu/DCLEM/ptgguide/ptggd7.htm
http://members.aol.com/jimb3d/rainbow/rainbow.html
http://clinton4.nara.gov/WH/glimpse/tour/html/green.html
http://www.bme.jhu.edu/labs/chb/faq/faq.html
http://faculty.washingon.edu/chudler/nosek.html
http://www.rgbworld.com/color.html

To order additional copies of
SAVE PERFECTION FOR

Heaven

Have your credit card ready and call:

1-877-421-READ (7323)

or please visit our web site at
www.pleasantword.com

Also available at: www.amazon.com

Printed in the United States
58221LVS00002B/1-51